INTEGRAL HALACHAH

Transcending and Including

Jewish Practice
Through the Lens of Personal Transformation
and Global Consciousness

RABBI ZALMAN SCHACHTER-SHALOMI

and

RABBI DANIEL SIEGEL

Trafford rev. 09/24/2021

 www.trafford.com
North America & international
toll-free: 844-688-6899 (USA & Canada)
fax: 812 355 4082

Cover Art
Transcending and Including

by David Friedman

Fractals are forms that are self-similar on different scales – like the nine-branched trees in this poster.

Notice how the branches of each fractal tree are similar to the shape of the Hebrew letter *Shin*. The letter *Shin*, which is comprised of three vertical lines, represents Fire or transcendence.

Transcendence has to do with growth and evolution. Look at the smallest tree and see how it is just a 'baby' sapling. As it grows, it transcends its previous limitations and becomes twice as large.

As this tree continues to mature, it transcends its limitations and grows twice its size again. As it grows further, it transcends itself again, and again, and again. But notice that all of the previous stages of development are included in the composite structure of the largest tree.

This is also true of human beings. As we grow and evolve in consciousness from egocentric Chaos to ethnocentric Torah to worldcentric Messianic awareness, we should transcend the limitations of the previous levels, but we should always include these less-inclusive states of being in the composite nature of our fully mature and integrated kosmic consciousness.

http://www.kosmic-kabbalah.com/index.htm

innerart@netvision.net.il

DEDICATION

In memory of my father,
Anton Joseph Fleischman (z"l),
and in honor of my mother,
Judith Anne Fleischman
with gratitude and love
for starting me on the spiritual pathway
that enriches my life
and led me to my beloved teacher Reb Zalman.

Catherine A. Dodi

TABLE OF CONTENTS

PREFACE i
    The Structure of this Book iii
    The Arba'a Turim iii
    Halachic Principles iv
    Reb Zalman's Thoughts vi
    מבוא לקורא עברית מאת ר' זלמן x

INTEGRAL HALACHAH: AN OVERVIEW 1
    "Who Has Chosen Us" 3
    Background Review 4
    "Halachah in the Red" 23
    The Transpersonal and Behavior 24
    Practical Considerations for Integral Halachah 27
    Reaching In 31
    What God Wants From Us 34

SHI'UR ONE: ELEMENTS OF INTEGRAL HALACHAH
.... 39
    A Modern Midrash 40
    Klal Yisra'el and Jewish Renewal 46
    Halachic Anchors 47
    Shared Values 54
    Organicity / Endoskeletal 59

SHI'UR TWO: ORACH CHAYYIM 69
    Davvenen: Birchot Ha-Shachar 69
    T'fillin 70
    Between Solo and Minyan 72
    Shabbat 74
    Yom Tov Sheni 80
    Appendix A: "From Solo to Minyan" 87
    Appendix B: Eating Kitniyot (Legumes) on Pesach 89

SHI'UR THREE: YOREH DE'AH 93
  Sh'chitah / Slaughtering 95
  Becoming Baki 101
  What a Rabbi Needs to Know 103
  From Issur to Hetter 105
  Mikveh 108
  Gerut 111
  Appendix: Eco-Kashrut 117

SHI'UR FOUR: EVEN HA-EZER 131
  Being a Jew Inside 131
  Marriage Contracts 137
  Loss of Trust 140
  Divorce Contracts 142
  Homosexuality 150
  Appendix: Modern Covenants Need A Modern Ketubah .....
  154

SHI'UR FIVE: CHOSHEN MISPHAT 159
  Appendix: Sacred Controversy 167

EPILOGUE 173

Preface

This publication of this book completes a major project in bringing the core teachings of Rabbi Zalman Schachter-Shalomi (Reb Zalman) into a form accessible to a new generation of readers as well as to those who have had the special opportunity to listen to him in person. The series begins with *Jewish with Feeling*, written in collaboration with Joel Segel. It is followed by *Credo of a Modern Kabbalist*, *The Kabbalah of Tikkun Olam*, *Renewal is Judaism Now!*, and this book, all written together with Rabbi Daniel Siegel.[1]

These books do follow a sequence and we recommend to the beginning student to read them in the order given above. Integral Halachah is designed for those who already have a background in Reb Zalman's concepts. We are assuming, therefore, that many of the basic Hebrew terms do not require explanation and we focus our explanatory notes and essays on the more advanced ideas and terms.

For many years, Reb Zalman has taught that the halachic process is essential to Judaism's ability both to adapt to new situations and maintain continuity with its past. At the same time, given the paradigm shift through which we are living, that process requires the addition of a major, new category in order to absorb the fundamental changes in world-view which now constitute a new set of basic assumptions. As Reb Zalman will say himself, this shift is symbolized by the photographs of our Earth taken from space. It is no longer possible to speak of an Earth centered universe and a Jewish centered history. As he said to me many years ago, we are now challenged to create a modern Judaism which is compelling without being fanatical, magnetic without being dogmatic.

---

[1] All the works cited here, as well as others, are available from the ALEPH ReSources Catalog, located on the ALEPH website (www.aleph.org).

Reb Zalman gave this new halachic category the name, "Psycho-Halachah." It means a *halachah* which incorporates and accepts the validity of personal experiential data in determining what changes from past practice have value. Whether a practice "works" or not is a legitimate consideration to add to those which are already present in the classical process developed during the last major paradigm shift at the time of the destruction of the Second Temple in Jerusalem and the two centuries or so afterwards (70CE-250CE). It recognizes that we are all now Jews by choice and our communities are voluntary ones.

In addition, a contemporary approach to *halachah* requires that we incorporate a recognition that there are many spiritual practices which contribute, individually and collectively, to the redemptive process. Judaism needs to be in a respectful and collaborative relationship with these traditions and paths, rather than in a hierarchical relationship with them. Also, the Jewish people needs to see its own future as bound together with that of all humankind. Therefore, we need to participate in the process of developing a universal consciousness as intrinsic to our particularity as is nurturing our uniqueness.

While Reb Zalman's student's and colleagues have agreed with the essentials of his ideas, we have had some concern over the name of Psycho-Halachah. With his permission and encouragement, we embarked on a consultative process to find a new name. In a way which exemplifies the value of the "consensus of the pious," an idea you will encounter more than once in the following pages, every person who made a suggestion made the same one, without consultation with each other. Thus emerged the name of "Integral Halachah," which is used now throughout this book.

The Structure of this Book

It is in two major sections. The first is an overview, given as a *shi'ur* in Boulder, Colorado at the Jewish Community Center on March 13, 2005. It was transcribed by Ruth Seagull and edited for this volume.

The second section is a set of *shi'urim* taped by Reb Zalman for the 1993 ALEPH Kallah. In his words, "It was a time of recuperation from surgery and I could not travel. With the help of Rabbi Gershon Winkler and his wife Lakme, we recorded this series of videotapes touching on various aspects of *halachah* The videotapes were then played for the Kallah attendees and the Winklers served as commentators."

There is an introductory *shi'ur* followed by four more, each focussing on a different unit of the *Shulchan Aruch*. Between each of these *shi'urim* is an essay on specific subjects from within that section. All of them are by Reb Zalman, except for one piece related to *kashrut* on Pesach and another short essay and primary sources concerning the use of mediation and arbitration in Jewish law, compiled by Daniel Siegel.

The Arba'a Turim

The four part division of codes of Jewish practice used by the author of the *Shulchan Aruch*[2] and many subsequent writers was initiated by Rabbi Jacob ben Asher (1270?-1340). It is based on the description of the high priest's "breastpiece of Judgment" which had four rows of three stones each (Exodus 28:13ff). In turn, the names he gave the divisions are also scriptural.

Orach Chayyim, the name of the first volume, relates to time-bound practices such as prayer and holy days, and comes from Psalm 16:11, where the Psalmist asks to be shown the way of

---

[2] Rabbi Joseph Karo in the 16th century.

living. The title of the second volume, *Yoreh De'ah* is from Isaiah
28:9. *Even HaEzer* is from I Samuel 7:12 and *Choshen Mishpat*
from Exodus 28:15. At the beginning of each *shi'ur*, Reb
Zalman summarizes the major subject areas of that *tur*.

Halachic Principles

The introduction of the category of Integral Halachah
does not mean that it replaces all the categories of classical
halachah. Reb Zalman has been very clear that his model is
inclusive and that new concepts need to be "backward
compatible." This means that Integral Halachah, like other
categories introduced at other times, is meant to simultaneously
transcend and include those that preceded it. We invoke it only
because, "seeing ourselves in the presence of the living God, we
want to strengthen the Jewish covenant while seeing ourselves
at the same time as stewards of the planet." Reb Zalman
identifies six areas addressed by Integral Halachah:

- It flows from a meaningful theology to which we
  can give credence

- It produces a doable *halachah* in harmony with
  the social agreements implicit in our society

- It is addressed to average people and provides a
  spiritual technology accessible to them as well as
  to advanced students and contemplatives.

- It is aware of other spiritualities, of both sister
  and nature religions, with which it is in
  conversation and exchange.

- It recognizes that we need forms of *kashrut* that
  complement and support ecological concerns.
  At the same time, our ecological concerns were
  challenged and informed by biblical laws which

protect the environment, such as *Sh'mittah*
(Sabbatical year), *Yovel* (the Jubilee), and other
laws connected with agriculture and animal
husbandry.

• While it is clear that we need to emphasize and
strengthen Shabbat observance in our social
milieu, the original interdictions concerning
work need to be updated by making some things
more lenient and others more stringent.[3]

Categories of classical *halachah* which inform the way
Integral Halachah develops include:

הוראת שעה: This is a "teaching for the hour," which is not
necessarily intended to set a lasting precedent. Invoking this
principle allows for experimentation to take place and for new
conclusions and consensus to emerge over time.

אין גוזרין גזירה על הצבור אלא אם כן רוב הצבור יכולין לעמוד
בה: You don't legislate what the community can't practice
(Talmud *Bavli Horayot* 3b).

מפני דרכי שלום: Literally, for the sake of the ways of peace,
which is the rationale given for a whole series of *halachot*
beginning in the Mishnah (primarily in *Gittin* ch. 5) and continuing
until the present.

תקנת הקהל: A community can legislate for itself using local
standards in a way which is binding.[4]

דרכיה דרכי נעם: "Her ways are pleasant" (Proverbs 3:17) is
invoked as a standard against which the viability of a practice
can be measured.

---

[3] Reb Zalman's words in text he sent to me to be included in this preface.

[4] Reb Zalman discusses this principle at greater length in the introductory
shi'ur in part two of this book.

All of the above are used most often *l-koola* / to be lenient. On the other side, a *chumra* / stringency which we endorse is that of actualizing the messianic transformation on the personal level now.[5]

Reb Zalman's Thoughts

This book is *torah she-b'al peh* / oral teaching, allowing for update and revision. It begins a discussion and introduces a process. At times, it may seem dry, but this is what is required to describe a modern halachic toolbox. We are assuming that you, dear reader, are already inspired and prepared to move to this next stage in the implementation of our shared vision.

I deal with the rubble of the holocaust, so please don't expect order and precision. Rather, join me in relating to ancient questions needing new answers in this time of paradigm shift. How do we find meaning by continuing to be Jews? After the holocaust, is God simply an abusive spouse? How do we connect to joy, to purpose, and why should we want to within a Jewish context, if it has been the cause of so much pain?

The only way I know how to answer these questions is by creating a new, transcending, Judaism which, while remaining loyal to the past and including it, goes beyond it and grows even larger. In other words, our practice must always reference the larger purpose of the Jewish people in the world, our commitment to God and to what we call *tikkun olam*, to being agents of redemption. We now also know that we are not alone in this commitment, but part of something greater, a sharing with other people and paths.

---

[5] Reb Zalman discusses this principle at greater length in Part One, pp. 34-36

Notes on Translation and Transliteration

Translations of verses from the Torah are taken from *The Five Books of Moses: A New Translation with Introductions, Commentary and Notes* by Everett Fox (NY; Schocken Books, 1995).

Translations of other biblical verses from Prophets and Writings are taken from *Tanakh: A New Translation of the Holy Scriptures According to the Traditional Hebrew Text* (Philadelphia; The Jewish Publication Society, 1985).

Transliterated Hebrew words are followed by a forward slash (/) and their translation. I have used a separate font (Times) to distinguish the translation from the continuation of the sentence.

Most of the time, we use the *s'phardic*, or modern Israeli pronunciation. At other times, we've left in the *ashkenazic* which comes more easily to Reb Zalman so that you can have a flavor of his voice.

Footnotes in which I add observations are marked (ds).

Footnotes where Seth Fishman added valuable observations are marked (srf).

Another function of footnotes is to call your attention to people who have taken Reb Zalman's suggestions and produced materials expressive of his vision.

Special Thanks From Daniel To...

Cathy Dodi, for the financial gift which assured this project, for her helpful suggestions and encouragement;

ALEPH's Executive Director, Debra Kolodny whose support for this work, both personally and through seeking grants, has been invaluable;

The Kellogg Foundation for a crucial grant to support the writing;

The many in ALEPH who supported me personally;

Seth Fishman, who lovingly transcribed the 1993 talks, helped edit them, and provided invaluable commentary, discussion, and questions all leading to greater clarity in the text. His love for Reb Zalman came through in the way most needed, in attention to every word and idea.

Reb Zalman himself, my rebbe for over thirty years and a creative force in my life for more than forty. It is such a privilege to share this process with him.

To my life partner, Hanna Tiferet, an extraordinary rabbi and teacher in her own right, who has shared this long journey of discovery and whose insights and contributions I have so deeply absorbed.

Rabbi Daniel Siegel
Hornby Island, British Columbia
On the day of Tiferet in G'vurah
5767

From Reb Zalman

When reading this book, please keep in mind how much work has gone into shaping this material. I join with Reb Daniel in thanking all the people listed above and the many others who contributed in ways that can no longer be credited by name. But most of all, the credit belongs to *HeChaver Harav Hadayan* Rabbi Daniel Siegel. Reb Daniel was the first person I ordained. He came with a background gained in various schools of higher Jewish learning and a rabbinic seminary. The sense of vocation he felt was not in harmony with the policies of the school he attended. Issues of human rights, the yearning for a simple natural life, the wish to pray at a much greater depth, the longing to acquire contemplative skills, all of these made him look for a mentor. I am blessed that he chose me and in turn that I chose him. Because from the start it was clear that we were colleagues in the task of renewing Judaism. Knowing the sources, he was able to fill in as well as to correct the citations needed to substantiate the thought expressed here.

The merit of bringing this collaboration to you the reader belongs to Reb Daniel. May God grant him robust health and the right livelihood so that he might bring his own work to a public that needs it.

מבוא לקורא עברית מאת ר' זלמן

מכל הברכות שחנני השי"ת היא הברכה של תלמיד הגון. בזה
הנני להציג עבודתו של תלמידי היקר הרב הדיין ר' דניאל
סג"ל. הוא כבר הראה חילו בעריכת ספרי *Credo of a Modern*
Kabbalist בו טרח לסדר את ההרצאות שלי מדיבור המשוטט
לסדר קריאה וגם טרח למצוא מראי מקומות ומסמכים מאוצרות
ומכמני מסורתנו כדי לעזור לתלמיד הקורא להבין ולהחשיב את
התוכן. הוא - יאריך השי"ת ימיו ושנותיו בנעימים מתוך בריות
גופא ונהורא מעליא - היה הראשון והבכור של התלמידים
שהסמכתי לרבנות. עליו כתבתי **תעודת–חבר** שאינו מוציא
מתחת ידו דבר שאינו מתוקן.

הוא בא אלי אחרי שנות לימודי תורה ויהדות בבתי ספר גבוהים
ובית מדרש לרבנים, כבר בר אוריון ויודע ספר. אבל כשבא
הביע לי מרת נפשו שלא מצא את עצמו בין מלמדיו מקודם כי
אף שמצא שם בקיאות וחריפות לא מצא שם את הנצוץ הרוחני
שלבו חפץ בו.

בעבודה זו הראה עוד כשרונותיו ובקיאותיו בספרות ההלכה
משתי בחינות: דרכי בענין התחדשות ההלכה לפי דרישת זמננו
וקהלנו אינה סלולה. דרכנו בהתחדשות היהדות בחילוף
העידונים אחרי השואה הנוראה ושנוי תפיסת הקיום (דברים
שעמדתי עליהם בספרון *ישמרו דעת* וב *Paradigm Shift*, ובספר
קרבת אלקים) הביאו אותי לתכנן שיטה של psycho-halakhic
process היינו! תהליך ההלכה התומך בבני עדתנו לשמירת
ההלכה באופן של קירוב לדבקות בה' ושל בחינת 'אתהפכא' –
טראנס־פורמציה של המדות. היו כמה פעמים אשר מתוך לחץ
התנאים נטינו יותר מן המדה או לצד זה או לצד כנגדו או
להחמיר לצד הדין או לצד צורכי צבור של אמונה.

וזאת צריך לְהֵאָמֵר: אין אנו מתרברבין לפסוק להלכה בעד
האדוקים בהלכה המקובלת. אנו יוצרים עמדה כ'הוה אמינא'
להבאים (א) מחוץ לחסות תחת כנפי המסורת ובזה נהיה
כפרוזדור ו(ב) לאלה שנתגדלו בסביבת שומרי תו"מ ולא מצאו
סיפוק נפש בעדתם עד שנתקשרו אתנו.

מטרתנו היתה בדרך כלל להתרכז לבחינות 'שלמות העבודה'
ולהקשיב ל'טעמי המצווֹת' כפי הבנתנו מפי ספרים וסופרים וגם
לכוון לבעיות הצבור שלנו. לכן כמה פעמים שנינו מהנוסח
והמנהג המקובל וההלכה הפסוקה של האחרונים אשר תנאיי
חייהם היו שונים מהתנאים שלנו.

Rabbi Zalman Schachter-Shalomi
Boulder, Colorado
On the eve of our redemption
Pesach 5767

PART ONE
INTEGRAL HALACHAH: AN OVERVIEW
Introduction

This is an overview of what I have been calling Psycho-Halachah and what we are now calling Integral Halachah. This concept is crucial for understanding the totality of Jewish Renewal and for bringing our deeper purpose into visibility through practice in this world. Some people mistakenly believe that involvement in Jewish Renewal means participating in "Judaism-Lite" – a practice which doesn't have too many calories, won't make you fat, and does not ask too much from you. The truth is that the paradigm shift through which we are traveling now raises issues that demand serious assessment. In the past, *halachah* meant **obligation**; it was something that bound us. All you needed to say was, "This is the *halachah*," and people would immediately recognize their involvement and that any deviation from it was a sinful transgression. Clearly, this is not the case today.

It is also true that, in the past, we interpreted paradigm shifts as being tragic. In some cases, such as the destruction of the temples, this was true. But, as I have said elsewhere,[1] shifts happen in ways which may be viewed as releasing creativity rather than being tragic. The vessels holding the light, our understanding of God and the ways in which the universe unfolds, fill and shatter from the accumulation of experience and new data, creating space for new vessels holding new understanding. For example, even though sacrificing animals in the Temple was once truly meaningful, I can't imagine anybody getting high on *Pesach* by eating a lamb they kept in the house for a few days, taking it to priests who slaughtered it, and catching the blood in vessels which was then poured on the altar.

---

[1] See *The Kabbalah of Tikkun Olam.*

On the other hand, even if this form no longer speaks to us, the question remains, "What was the purpose of this ritual and what was its effect on us supposed to be?" It is one thing for a ritual to lose its meaning, but losing what that ritual was supposed to accomplish is much more serious. That loss of meaning could remove something so basic from our spiritual lives that we would be in trouble. If the old ritual can no longer transform us, and we have no replacement for it, then that would be a very sad situation.

So I want to begin this essay with a prayer:

> You commanded us,
> You,
> You commanded us
> to exercise our awareness in Your Torah.
> For this instruction
> we offer You, our God, our appreciation.
> We ask that we may find zest and delight
> in the words of your teaching.
> May we and our children and their children too
> become intimate with You,
> and with pure intent
> immerse ourselves in the Torah.
> *Baruch Atah YAH.*
> You mentor Your people in Torah.
> *Baruch Atah YAH,*
> I offer you my thanks, Cosmic Majesty
> and worship You
> for selecting us from among all nations
> to reveal to us that Torah which is meant for us..
> *Baruch Atah YAH,*
> You keep gifting us with Your Torah.

"Who Has Chosen Us"

People often misunderstand what we mean when we talk about the Jews being chosen or special. What I believe and expressed by formulating this blessing as I did, is that the Torah which is given to us fits our spiritual DNA. It's clear that for other peoples, living under different conditions and with their own way of feeling the earth, that the way the earth under their feet speaks manifests in forms of religion which fit their spiritual DNA. Therefore, when we say that this religious form is meant for us, we're not saying that it's better or worse.

For example: suppose the same doctor prescribed medications for both a cancer and heart patient under his/her care. Now, imagine that they switched prescriptions and each one took the other person's medicine. It's obvious that this wouldn't work, even though each medicine is appropriate for one of the patients. It says in the Talmud that the Torah is meant to be *k-sam chayyim* / like an elixir of life for us, an antidote for the poison of the *yetzer ha-ra*. The Talmud continues by calling Torah *tavlin*,[2] meaning a pickling spice to marinate in. In other words, the inclination we have for selfishness and evil is not so bad; it depends on what marinade it's in. Without directed selfishness, a person wouldn't be motivated to do much of anything. Alan Watts used to say that love means to say to someone, "I love you with the purest selfishness." When the Torah says, *"V-a'havta et Ha-shem Elohecha b-chol l-vav'cha u-v-chol nafsh'cha u-v-chol m'odecha* / Love God with all your heart, soul, and might," it means the same thing – we love God with the purest selfishness.

---

[2] *Talmud Bavli Kiddushin* 30b.

Background Review

In order to truly begin, I need to review some foundational ideas. These are the underpinnings of classical *halachah* and you need to understand them before we can start to talk about what changes are needed. Please follow along and my direction will soon become clear.

The foundation of the halachic process that we inherited takes its cue from the book of Deuteronomy. The Hebrew name of this fifth book of the Torah is often given as *Mishneh Torah*, which means a repeat, review, or a second giving of the law. Now, why should the law have to be given again? What makes this transmission different from that which is recorded in the previous three books? In Deuteronomy, Moses gives us the law like a person who is scolding children. It's as though his preface is, "You *shmegegs*, you backsliders. I've had *tsores* / troubles shlepping you around for all these years. I'm telling you! Don't you move to the right, don't you move to the left. Do exactly as I tell you!"

A little later in chronological time, we find the following attributed to King Solomon in the book of *Kohelet* / Ecclesiastes: There is a time for everything; a time to do, a time not to do.[3] Now things are seen as shifting and changing, no longer absolute. Things have become dynamic. This is a very important point.

Just before the US presidential election in 2004, George Lakoff came out with a book called *Don't Think of an Elephant*.[4] In it, he claims that the single most important reason for Republican election victories was their success in framing the

[3] Ch 3.:1ff. Scholars assume that the Book of Deuteronomy was written during the time of the divided kingdom before the destruction of the first Temple, while *Kohelet* is likely a scroll from the second Temple period.

[4] Chelsea Green Publishing Company, 2004. George Lakoff is Professor of Linguistics at the University of California, Berkeley.

national debate. This ability was more significant than any other advantage they had, including financial. They were so good at imposing this frame on the American mind that people could no longer think outside it. Even Democrats found themselves responding and defending themselves within the parameters of the Republican frame. At the core of this framing is the image of the strong father who is "in charge." On the national level, it means that there is a great white father in Washington who, like the Pope speaking ex cathedra, is infallible and does not make mistakes. He therefore remains credible even when he asks people to agree to do that which is not really good for them. Lakoff argues that the only way to reverse this effect is to change the frame, to get people thinking in a different way about the issues.

Using this approach, let's ask what kind of frame the book of Deuteronomy provides? In the Book of Proverbs, also attributed to King Solomon, we find the saying, "*Shma bni mussar avicha v-al titosh torat imecha* / Listen, my son to the reproof of your father and do not put aside, forsake, the Torah of your mother."[5] What I hear in this aphorism is that the same Torah appears to some people as being *mussar avicha* and to others as *torat imecha*. Those for whom it is *mussar avicha* see Torah in the Deuteronomic frame as something which one must always do. Those for whom it is *torat imecha* see it in the light of yet another aphorism, "*D'racheha darchei no'am* / Her ways are ways of pleasantness."[6] This approach focuses less on the absolute nature of the commandments and more on those parts of Torah which deal with *shalom bayit* / peace at home, such as caring for the poor and the disadvantaged. Thus, the same Torah looks different, is framed differently, depending on which side of this aphorism you choose.

---

[5] Ch. 1:8.

[6] ibid, 3:16.

Shifting the Balance

With the advent of feminism and its mind, I sense that Jewish Renewal's approach to Torah needs to shift the balance from *mussar avicha* as primary to giving more emphasis to *torat imecha*. The frame in which it is Papa who who tells you what do is heteronomy; that is to say, *hetero nomos*, the law is imposed by someone else, a God who descends on a mountain and delivers commandments. Today, we have to shift more to the side of autonomy, in which we determine what is right for us to do. When we can give full consent to something and take the initiative, then it's ours and our commitment to it is stronger.

In the past, when we lived in small villages and urban ghettos, the heteronomic idea worked well for us. We lived in very close proximity to one another and the ways available for earning a living were restricted by laws. These prevented us from dong most crafts and forced us into a very limited number of professions, such as money-lending. That meant also that there was real pressure from outside in addition to the pressures from inside oneself. If you live in a ghetto and everybody knows your business, then there is no way you can do anything else than be a Jew. There was no way for an individual to choose which parts of Jewish practice s/he wanted to fulfill and which not. The only option was either to buy in to the whole package or give up being Jewish altogether by getting baptized. So, on the one hand, you were stuck, and, on the other, you belonged. You were not a Jew by choice. Today, everyone is a Jew by choice, even those who are born Jews. This brings me back to the issue of autonomy through a historical route; everybody is now in that situation of having to choose whether or not to be Jewish and, if yes, how Jewish to be.[7]

---

[7] See the first chapters of *Credo of a Modern Kabbalist* for a more detailed description of how this choice works itself out.

Finding the Norm

If acknowledging that autonomy has to become a more important contributor to halachic decision-making, then finding its counterpart, namely the communal norm, becomes more difficult than it was in the past. Despite the fact that the books map out and describe what one does from the moment the eyes open in the morning, from saying *modeh ani*, until the last words of *ha-mappil* at night, after which one mustn't talk until the morning again, in truth the book still does not cover every possible behavior. There is still a social element that I call the consensus of the committed, or the consensus of the pious. That consensus has always been somewhat different for each group of Jews and even for each community. That consensus was much easier to identify in a heteronomic, small community based Judaism than it can be in the more autonomous Jewish life of today.

It is so interesting to notice how even the consensus within homogenous Jewish communities has become a lot freer than it used to be. For example, on *Shabbat* I can go to one of the Orthodox *minyanim* here in Boulder where everybody knows that I didn't walk from home. Yet, they will still call me to the Torah and sometimes allow me to participate as *ba'al t'fillah*. The reason is that without me, there wouldn't have been a *minyan* at all. The consensus of that *minyan* there assembled is that completing itself is a higher value than the observance levels of the individuals who make it up. Therefore, the usual standards by which you determine the suitability of someone for leadership or an honor can be waived. In this case at least, the consensus of the pious is contracted to that particular small group from the larger, and clearly stated, consensus of the Orthodox rabbinate which you can find in the books. What makes this especially interesting is that it is not explicit but implicit. That's a very important distinction, because while the book, the heteronomous teaching, may be and in this case at least is clearly explicit, we're all complicit in creating that implicit way that we call the consensus of the pious.

If we want to be able to create something like Integral Halachah, that is to say to build a new approach to *halachah* that remains compatible with our past, we first have to do something that's called deconstruction. This is hard to do because the people who are inside the father *mussar* thing and for whom it is the only meaningful way to practice, will and do deny our right to do this. They question who we think we are, believing that we are arrogant and rebellious. If the Father God hasn't explicitly sanctioned this from above, then it shouldn't be done at all. However, if our goal is to take responsibility for our consciousness, behavior, and covenant with God, then we have to say that not only do we have the right, but it's a *mitzvah*. In working these things out, we fulfill the *mitzvah* of asking, "*Mah ha-shem Elohecha sho'el mei-imcha* / What is it that God is asking of us [today]?[8]

It's so interesting to notice that this need to ask what it is that God wants from us today exists even in worlds where people believe that literal scripture is all that is needed. I'm thinking of stories about how Evangelical Christians are starting to ask this same question and which led one of their leaders to buy a hybrid car because he had grown concerned about air pollution. In this case, too, the questioning resulted in a change of behavior, a new halachic modeling, and an understanding that driving a conventional car is no longer "eco-kosher."

What is it that give us the right to deconstruct? The answer is because we have been given greater insight and consciousness than people had in the past. After Freud, it is no longer possible to live without being introspective and transpersonal. We are

---

[8] Deuteronomy 10:12.

required, if you will, to figure out why we do things, how was something done in the past, and what was any given practice supposed to do for the practitioner. We now ask what was the inner gestalt of a particular *mitzvah*, separate from its outer form. What we want and need to know is how did it create transformation in a person.

For instance, at the beginning of the book of Leviticus, Moses is standing outside the just-completed tabernacle because the Presence of God is so overwhelming that he can't go in. Then, "*Va-yikra el Mosheh* / [God] called to Moshe" and began to tell him what to do in that building that has just been dedicated. God says, "*Adam ki yakriv mi-kem korban l-adonai* / A human being, if he will offer **of himself** a sacrifice unto God." That's the introduction. But then God says, "I'll do you a favor, I'll take a sheep instead." Do you see what happens here? The opening line tells us that what we have to give is of our being, our substance. If you're in a shepherd culture, then your substance is sheep. So the practical implication of "giving of oneself" becomes offering an animal on the altar. Continuing in the same vein as in the previous paragraph, what we now need to ask is what happens in our situation today, where money has become the primary "substance" which represents our material being. How then do we offer of this substance and what is the "altar" on which it is given?

This is not a new question, of course, since it has been asked ever since the Temple was destroyed. One common answer to the question is that we give of our money in place of sacrificing animals. What I have come to realize is that simply giving is not really enough. In order for the inner transformative purpose to be fulfilled, there needs to be some way in which the receiving is as important as the giving and that there is some relationship between the giver and recipient.

One year, Reb Naftoli Ropshitser came home after giving his annual and long *drashah* on *Shabbat ha-Gadol*.[9] His wife, the *rebbetzin*, asked him how the *drashah* went. He answered, "I achieved half of my goals." She asked, "What did you preach about, that you were only half successful?" He replied, "My main point was that the rich should help the poor make Pesach. I achieved half my goals because the poor agreed with me right away. I succeeded in convincing the poor to accept help from the rich!"

I want to emphasize that the point of this story for me is that the transformative quality of the *mitzvah* is what we are looking to preserve. On the one hand, this can require us to rethink an old practice and, on the other, we need to be able to ensure that the relationship which makes the transformation possible can happen. In each situation, then, I ask what it was that was supposed to happen through this practice.

Another example is how do we deal with guilt today now that we no longer have sacrifices? Do the things we do go deep enough? Do they really bring about change in us?

When I ask myself how a particular practice began, I find that it often begins with somebody having an insight. Jacob is leaving home to escape his brother's anger. He sleeps "in that place" at night and has the amazing dream of a ladder reaching to heaven on which angels are going up and coming down. He says, "This must be God's house." And, because it's God's house, he needs to mark this place in some special way. So he puts up a marker of rocks where our tradition says the temple is built much later on. Now, he wants to mark the stone itself, so that it is obvious that the place is sacred. If he marked it by pouring water over it, it would dry up right away and no

---

[9] Traditionally, in Europe especially, rabbis gave two longer and carefully prepared talks each year, one on the *Shabbat* before *Yom Kippur* and the other on the *Shabbat* before Passover, called *Shabbat haGadol* / the great Sabbath.

one would recognize how special the place is. But oil is different, so he puts oil on the stone which will leave a longer lasting impression. This was his insight and the way that he gave it expression.

This insight was strong enough to inspire people who came later to follow and build on it. Over time, they created what we call a *minhag* / custom. Since *minhag* is the way we conduct ourselves, gradually the *minhag* becomes law. This is how society creates a way of traffic control. It says the best way not to bump into each other is that we should all zig and zag together and, if we have rules about that, then everyone will know how to move. The softness of insight becomes more solid – a custom becomes a very strong, solid law.

Another way of looking at this same process is to imagine a conversation between Moses and God on Mount Sinai. When they begin to discuss the form which Israelite worship should take, Moses invokes the principle of *"ma'aseh avot siman l-vanim /* What our ancestors did is a good model for the children to follow."* He then asks if it would be okay for "his" Israelites to do as their ancestors did, namely to give expression to their commitment to live out the meaning of their experience of the Divine, this time through animal sacrifice in a temple. And, if so, would God guarantee that the Divine flow be stimulated by their sacrifices just as it was by those of the ancestors, when it was spontaneous, powerful, and transformative. In other words, in spite of the fact that it will now become a routine, dear God, would You agree that this can still be so? In Latin they would call this *ex opere operatum*, the fact of performing the action recreates the original situation. God agrees and so what the ancestors did is assigned to the children.

But, what happens when we are no longer able to follow the form which our ancestors used? In the case of animal sacrifice as the primary form of worship, what happens when the temple is destroyed? What happens when the people themselves begin to feel that the traditional form no longer works for them? At that point, we need to ask again what was the essence of the insight from which the practice emerged and consider creating a link between the same insight and a new or different practice.

The first chapter of the Book of Ezekiel describes his inaugural vision. Ezekiel saw a wheel in the middle of the air which later was described as the *merkavah*. To us, *merkavah* would be a vehicle. But a vehicle doesn't necessarily mean something with four wheels. Rather, we can understand it as an instrumentality. The best metaphor I have for this is a ventriloquist's dummy, which becomes the vehicle for the ventriloquist. The difference between the metaphor and the reality is that the dummy can't help himself while we have freedom of choice. When I feel a mandate coming from the living God to which I want to respond, I say,"Dear God, I'm willing for You deploy me in any way You want. I offer myself as a vehicle for Your will." But it is still up to me to discover exactly what that willingness means on a daily basis. If I then use Abraham as my model and see what it was that he did, I discover that the core of his service was inviting guests into his home and offering hospitality; he was an instrument for *chesed / love*. If *ma'aseh avot siman l-vanim*, then I can be God's vehicle by copying the essence of the way Abraham lived out his willingness, rather than by emulating his way of building altars and sacrificing animals. This is how a modern person becomes a vehicle for God. What is central is that Abraham and Sarah and their children established the covenantal relationship between humans and God. They chose to become vehicles for God and that tells us that we too can be vehicles.[10]

---

[10] See *Torat M'nachem* (Mendel Schneerson), Vol. VI, 5712, Part 3:177 for a reference to this principle in a way which serves as the foundation for the dialogue Reb Zalman has created.

The next question has to do with developing a deep understanding of the many *mitzvot* that we have. These are the actions through which we continue to both express our commitment and reinforce it. One thing we find is that there are *mitzvot* which connect to a lot of instinctual things that we do. Let's take eating as a first example. When I feel hungry and want to eat, I first must make a *brachah*. So, before I actually put any food in my mouth, I'm required to become conscious of what I'm doing and connect my instinctual behavior to the Divine.

In just about every piece of instinctual behavior, we have a "stop" exercise that says: become conscious of what you're doing, make a *brachah*, socialize what you're doing. When you harvest a field, leave some for the poor. Every *mitzvah* embodies the message that filling an instinctual need cannot be done just by unthinking instinct alone! *Mitzvot tz'richot kavvanah*, a *mitzvah* demands that you come to awareness, that you wake up. It is when that happens that the *mitzvah* is full, it's right. *Kallah b-lo brachah assurah l-va'alah k-nidah* / A bride is forbidden to her bridegroom if they haven't said the *brachot* at the *chuppah*, that congress as an instinctual behavior alone is something not kosher. So you get the idea that there is a stop exercise before you go instinctual; think about what you are doing, socialize.

It's the same thing when you bake bread for Shabbat. We now call the whole loaf "*challah*," but at one time this word referred to one piece of dough over which one made a *brachah* and then baked separately.[11] This little piece of bread is then given to the local *kohen* / priest or burnt.[12] In our house we don't burn it, because I'm a *kohen* and I get to eat it. But, I eat it with a certain kind of consciousness, because the *kohen* who

---

[11] The *brachah* is: *Baruch atah Adonai Eloheinu melech ha-olam asher kid'shanu b-mitzvotav v-tzivanu l-hafrish challah.*

[12] We put it out for the birds to eat unless Reb Zalman was visiting. (ds)

receives the *challah* has to be like an altar. So when I eat the *challah* I pray, "*Ribbono shel Olam*, this is a holy act that I'm doing. Just like in the past, *kohanim* ate certain portions of the sacrifices while others were burnt on the altar, so today I am eating this *challah* as though it were a sacrifice to You."

In many ways, *tz'dakah* is the most obvious and most important example. Both before you begin to pray and even in the middle of prayer, one gives *tz'dakah*. Before starting to pray, first *yahev p'rutah l-ani* / let him give *tzedakah* to someone poor and then davven.[13] And in the middle of praying, near the end of *p'sukei d-zimra*, many communities have the custom of giving *tz'dakah*. Sharing one's wealth through giving *tz'dakah* is a basic element of how we make *halachah* for ourselves.

We begin with a model that has come down to us from the past and which has organic connection to the past. So if someone in the present wants to create a new custom for a new situation which has no roots in the past, it wouldn't feel Jewish. For instance, putting on a seat belt was just a secular thing until I reminded myself that the Torah says that one is obligated to build a fence to enclose the flat roof of a house so no one can fall down.[14] The Torah requires us to construct and use a safety mechanism. Now, when I get into the car, I say the *brachah*, "*asher kidshanu b'mitzvotav v'tzivanu al mitzvat ma'akeh* / who has commanded us about the mitzvah of a fence." I'm observing the same *mitzvah*, but in a new application. My issue may not be a flat roof, but the reason, "*pen yippol ha-nofel* / so that a person won't fall" and be injured, is also true for wearing a seat-belt. Our approach is to root whatever new thing we're doing organically to the past so that it has a connection.

---

[13] Talmud *Bavli Bava Batra* 10a. Rabbi *El'azar* would give *tz'dakah* and then pray.

[14] Deuteronomy 22:8.

The question now becomes whether we have the right to do such a thing. To explain this, I'll need to undermine the Papa frame a little bit. The Torah says very clearly, "Don't burn any fires in all your dwellings on the Sabbath day."[15] Taken literally, one would go around before every Shabbat and quench every lit fire. Now, if you live in an agricultural society in a warm country, that's not so bad. But what happens when there is cold weather or when people need to stay up after dark, at least once a week? During the week in a poor household, when you need oil for food, you may have one oil lamp so you can find your way around in the dark for a short time. But, for the most part, you go to bed when it gets dark. On Friday night, however, it is only by staying up a bit later that you can really enjoy a relaxed dinner. So the *chachamim* / wise ones, said two things. First, it's okay to have light after *Shabbat* begins as long as you light it before dark. Second, where during the week you might have one light, on *Shabbat* you have to have two. Then they did a really wonderful thing. They said that since the *Shabbat* command is given in both versions of the ten commandments, once as *shamor* / guard and once as *zachor* / remember, each of the lights corresponds to one of those ways of keeping Shabbat. It's like when my Mama would say, eat a spoonful for the *bobbe* / grandmother. Then the rabbis added another reason, that having the two candles will help there be *shalom bayit*, peace and harmony in the family.[16]

So, the question I asked earlier has been asked before and answered. Even though the Torah says clearly that you shouldn't have any fire burning on *Shabbat*, the *chachamim* changed this to mean that you shouldn't light a fire on *Shabbat*. But if you light it before *Shabbat* and it continues to burn after *Shabbat* begins, then it now becomes a *mitzvah*. Therefore, one has to be very careful around these lights and there is a whole

---

[15] Exodus 35:3.

[16] Isaiah Leib Horowitz, *Shnei Luchot Ha-Brit, Masechet Shabbat, Ner Mitzvah*, 4.

section in the Talmud dealing with what materials may be used for *Shabbat* lights. "*Ba-meh madlikin u-vameh ein madlikin* / **What oils may you use for lighting and what oils can you not use**," what kind of wicks may you use and what kind of wicks you don't use.[17] The reason for these prescriptions is to make sure that you don't have to mess with the wick and the oil on *Shabbat, shemma yatteh* / **lest you err**. It's important to get the lights set up so that there is no need to make any adjustments to the flame once *Shabbat* has begun.

Now, the fundamentalists of that time challenged this kind of rabbinic innovation. Who gives you the right to do this, to change the literal and obvious meaning of the Torah? What is this new idea of lighting candles? So the *chachamim* responded with an idea that has come to be seen as elegant. They quoted a verse in Psalms that says, "*Eit la-asot la-shem heferu toratecha.*" Literally, this verse means that it is time to act for God because they (the people) have abrogated your Torah. The rabbis accepted that meaning, but said the verse also could be translated to mean, "Because it is time to do something for God – abrogate the Torah!"[18] Sometimes you have to flip the meaning of Torah from the way it had been read in the past.

It doesn't say in the Torah that we should light candles for *Shabbat* and yet we say, "Who has commanded us to light." "*Heichan tzivanu?*" The rabbis ask. "Where is it written that we have to light candles?" We give ourselves the right to require this blessing over our changes, but we also agree that these changes need to anchored in the Torah somehow. Then they say, it is written that when you don't know what the law is, go up to Jerusalem and ask the priests and judges of your time.

---

[17] Mishnah *Shabbat* Ch. 2, read every Friday evening between *Kabbalat Shabbat* and *Ma'ariv* in many communities.

[18] Psalm 119:126 and Talmud *Bavli B'rachot* 63a.

Further, you had better do what they tell you to.[19] And why should this be so? Because, as *Moshe Rabeinu* said to Pharaoh, "*Va-anachnu lo neda mah na'avod et Hashem ad bo'enu shamah* / We won't know how to serve God till we get there."[20] Now, the rabbinic argument concludes, we've arrived at another new place and precedent alone, what we have learned from the past, is no longer enough and we have to consult with the living authorities of our time.

Another example of rabbinic precedent for changing the literal meaning of scripture comes from the laws concerning the sabbatical year. The Torah states that owners can cultivate their fields for six years at a time. Every seventh year, all fields are to lie fallow and anyone can come and take what they need. In addition, no debts can carry over a sabbatical year and outstanding balances are cancelled.[21] This was an important innovation during the biblical period when Israelite society was primarily agricultural, because the sabbatical year cancellation of debt prevented them from falling into feudalism. The Torah knows of this possibility through its telling of the story of Joseph, in which the Egyptian people had to sell themselves as slaves to Pharaoh for seed money during the seven years of famine. You find the same situation in medieval Europe where the people who once owned the land became sharecroppers, and sometimes even slaves, on the same land which had once belonged to them.

What Hillel did was to create a new weave which remained within the law. Rather than simply create a new law and throw the old one away which doesn't work because it breaks the continuity, he made a distinction between private debts and public debts. The kind of debts the Torah meant to be

---

[19] Deuteronomy 17: 8-11.

[20] Exodus 10:26.

[21] Deuteronomy 15:1-2.

cancelled at the sabbatical year are private, those where one person helps another out of a tough situation, usually because they already know each other well. Public debt, such as business loans, do not have to be cancelled. Therefore, if the two parties have a document written by a court to that effect, the money owing can carry over the sabbatical year. This made it possible for business loans to be contracted when needed, regardless of how close it was to the sabbatical year. Hillel's innovation made a freer movement of capital possible, so that Jews could participate in the international economy of that time. And he did this by using the existing law rather than abrogating it.

These are two situations among many from early rabbinic law. Let's take another example from a later time. At first, anyone could be a *shochet* / slaughterer of animals. In the days when everyone owned some goats and sheep, it wasn't practical to have one professionally trained *shochet* for a large area. So Jewish law had clearly stated instructions for anyone who needed to dispatch one of his animals. In fact, even in our time this has happened and I trained someone in Oregon who kills his own animals and will also do so for his neighbors. And, at one time, I wanted all the rabbis to whom I gave *semicha* to at least know how to slaughter birds.

On the whole, however, we know that this is no longer true. The law has shifted, so that now only a specially trained person can be a *shochet*. At one time, one could use any kind of knife, as long as it was sharp and free of nicks. Today, it can only be a special kind of knife, prepared in a special way. Now, this is good, because it means that, on this level at least, the laws of *sh'chitah* / ritual slaughter have kept up with changes in technology. In fact, when Reb Schneur Zalman learned about Swedish hollow ground blades, he so appreciated the improvement they represented over each *shochet* having to smithy his own knives that he ruled that they should be used.

He did this over the opposition of the Vilna rabbinic authorities, even though these *sakkinim m'lutashim*, as they were called, actually made the meat more kosher. I think their opposition stemmed from this being a change that they had not initiated.

From this example one can see that the changes are not always toward leniency. Sometimes, the changes are to make the law more stringent or exact and follow on changes in technology. In other words, changes in the world outside of the purely Jewish can trigger changes in *halachah*.

Let's return to the laws of *Shabbat* and apply this same approach to the cessation from work itself, its core concept. The Torah says that you must not do any *m'lachah* / work, but gives only hints and limited examples about how work is defined. This defining became the task of the rabbis, who had to bridge between the simple, agricultural economy of biblical times and the emerging, more mercantile economy of the Roman period. For them, the way to define work was to make a list of major categories, extracted from the work performed to build and maintain the Temple, as well as with agricultural tasks. Then, questions around whether other tasks were permitted or forbidden on *Shabbat* were resolved by deciding into which of these major areas the detail fit. Over time, the laws of *Shabbat* proliferated and a modern question is whether you can open a refrigerator if that makes the light go on or if it causes the thermostat to turn on the motor which starts cooling again. So, by following the classical line of reasoning in an incremental way, they have been led to make *Shabbat* clocks for these things and some people unscrew the light bulb before *Shabbat*. What you see is the result of a process of refinement which can lead to a burdensome complexity which discourages people from observing.

Let's focus in on the concept of work on *Shabbat* from a different angle. In general, what all the different categories of work seem to have in common is that the outcome, rather than the activity, is central. I'm doing this not because I want to do it myself, but because I need the product. Even the prohibition against writing can be explained in this way, since most people couldn't write and therefore took what needed to be written to a professional scribe. In the past, I may have done this kind of work myself, because people spent most of their time doing the basic chores which kept them afloat. In our economy, the equivalent is any job which I'm just as happy to delegate to another. It is something which has to get done and, if I can, I'll pay someone to do it. This is the kind of work that should not be done on *Shabbat* in the money economy in which we live.

We began with deconstruction, seeking to uncover the original insight which led to the creation of the practice which, in turn, is supposed to serve the purpose of helping us to remain connected to that insight. When we get into reconstruction, we need to go beyond social and historic reconstruction. What we really want is to re-create the same kind of situation, appropriate to our technology, our mind space, and how we can do it right.

Professor Mordechai Kaplan, the founder of Reconstructionism, formulated his approach to Judaism in the nineteen-thirties. In his day, pragmatism was at the core of how he approached Jewish peoplehood. He said that having a building whose only use was as a *shul* wasn't practical and that what was needed was a *beit k'nesset* / multi-purpose gathering place. Instead of building a "temple," build a *Beit Am*, a Jewish Center. In that building, there should be a place where liturgy is celebrated, but don't use that space only for prayer. Use it for concerts and lectures; have folding doors so part of the room can be a social hall and even include a gym. This was his way of deconstructing and then reconstructing. And, while this was useful and was implemented as Jews moved to suburbs, something was missing. That was the feeling we get walking into a church where there is an aroma of incense in a room which is softly lit, with stained glass windows and a light near the altar. It's a space where you walk on tiptoe and whisper. That sense of awe and mystery when entering a sanctuary was no longer there. In simple terms, this was because Reconstructionism has a low ceiling and doesn't deal comfortably with higher and spiritual things. When asked what God means, Professor Kaplan would say that God is the guarantor of values. Now this is a good and true thing as far as it goes, but notice how social it is and how it doesn't talk about spirituality. "God is the power that makes for salvation" was the highest level to which he could go, but what salvation meant to him was to live a good life here on earth, without any reference to what is beyond our individual lives.

We need to transcend the social and historic in our designing of the integral *halachah* for our time. We have to bring in the transpersonal and be aware of the paradigm shift. Sometimes I think that people come to Jewish Renewal services only because they enjoy them. They are more *freilich* / joyous, more exciting. People sing and dance, they hug each other – all these are wonderful things. And they think that this is how it always has been, because they are coming into Jewish Renewal now and weren't part of its birth pangs, of what we went through until we got to where we are now. So, it is truly important to understand that the paradigm shift is about a different way of thinking and of seeing ourselves in the world. It means being post triumphalist. It means that we no longer compare ourselves to non-Jews and that we are neither better nor worse than others. It means that non-Jews are not around just to be *Shabbat goyim*, as it were, and in our service.[22] It means that many things have shifted in our awareness, in our mind. And, if this truly is our new situation, then we need to go beyond the limitations that the old system now imposes so that we can, again, practice in a way that leads to transformation.

All of us who have worked even a little on our inner life feel a need for transformation. We feel an inertia that keeps us down, in a trance, asleep. It's an inertia that keeps us making the same mistakes over and over again, even though we get so angry at ourselves each time it happens. What we know we have to do is to transform, but how? Give me the right lever and I can lift the whole world, but what is the lever for transformation? To transform ourselves is like changing a car's tires while you're driving.[23] This metaphor makes clear how difficult this is. On the one hand, I have to go deep within in order to transform and, at the same time, I have to continue steering the vehicle which is my life. No one else can do the transforming for me; it is something I have to work on myself. If I don't practice, then it's not going to happen. And, if I have to be the person who can change me, how do I manage that when I can't stop my life from continuing to unfold at the same time? It means that, somehow, I have to reach out to forces and powers that are greater than I. Even self transformation cannot be done by myself alone. I need what we call *siya'ata di-shmaya* / heaven's aid.

Social and Historical Changes

There are social as well as individual changes which are mandated by the paradigm shift. For example, the reason the rabbis gave for not calling women to the Torah was *k'vod ha-*

---

[22] The *Shabbat Goy* was a non-Jew who would come into Jewish homes on *Shabbat* and stoke the furnace or light lights, doing for Jews what they couldn't do for themselves on *Shabbat*.

[23] Attributed to Susan Saxe, chief operating officer of ALEPH.

tzibbur / the **honor of the congregation**. It is not fitting for the congregation that a woman should have an *aliyah*.[24] This is still true in societies that are homo-social. To this day, women don't drive in societies like those of Saudi Arabia and Yemen; there is *purda* / **separation**. In homo-social societies, you see men holding hands as they walk. We might interpret that as homosexual, but it is not. Arab leaders kiss each other because that's the way things are done; that's how you grease the social wheels.

We no longer live in a homo-social, but hetero-social society, where men and women work and socialize together. The question for us is whether *k'vod ha-tzibbur* is satisfied when women are called up to the Torah. Sharing the *davvening* and Torah reading together is our way to honor the congregation.

"Halachah in the Red"

As I intimated earlier, today we are all Jews by choice. A good example of how this works is what I call *"Halachah* in the red and American kosher." Some time ago, I participated in a symposium in Commentary magazine about *halachah* and *kashrut*. I wrote the following scenario:

> Imagine a person going out to a restaurant. The server says that they have a special on pork chops. The person declines the special because s/he doesn't eat unclean animals and instead chooses beef. The server says that they do have steak, and would s/he like to have a pat of butter on the steak? The customer again declines the butter because s/he doesn't mix meat and milk. Then the server says that I forgot to tell you that we also

---

[24] Calling a woman would imply that there were no men present who could read from the Torah. See Talmud *Bavli M'gillah* 23a.

have a trout special. The customer says that this is
perfect and will have the fish instead of the steak.

Notice how this person made choices that are not in what
might be called "*hahachah* in the black." It's not like s/he went
to a kosher restaurant and ordered a kosher meal. The person
is in a non kosher restaurant and the choices s/he is making
along the way are choices that take the *halachah* of *kashrut* into
consideration. Yet, in spite of making these choices, s/he still is
eating on plates that are used for other food. It's not that s/he is
an unhalachic person but, as far as Orthodox people are
concerned, this is "*halachah* in the red," not the black. S/he has
a deficit to that law, but still is in the game. S/he is paying
attention and is thinking about *kashrut*. This is what Rabbi
Lawrence Kushner meant when he coined the expression,
"American Kosher." What he means is that you eat fish in a
non-kosher restaurant and you check whether the soup is made
from a vegetarian or meat stock. This leads to a consensus of
the committed in our circles of the minimum standards for
American Kashrut.

The Transpersonal and Behavior

There are four levels to the brain. A lot of *halachah* has been
directed to that one part of the brain associated with what
people would call behaviorism. There was a great teacher in
Jerusalem, Professor Yeshayahu Leibowitz, who argued that
Jewish practice had little to do with setting the stage for an
experience of God. Rather, the simple observance of *halachah*,
since that in and of itself is the submission to the Divine will, is
the closest we can come to a direct experience of God. The
way in which I understand this position is that most people
don't understand what the transpersonal really is about. They
think that transpersonal psychology doesn't take changing
behavior into consideration. Often, when I want to break a
habit, if you will, or an addiction, I have to begin by going cold

turkey. That's behaviorism, the ground, for the world of *Assiyah*. Therefore, in this approach, becoming a God centered person is a matter of changing one set of behaviors for another and *halachah* provides the new set.

However, in the end, this is not enough. At some point I have to ask what function the behavior which I need to change was serving, and that takes me to the world of feeling, to *Y'tzirah*. In *Y'tzirah*, I want to go into psychoanalysis or some other form of therapy. Next, I need to ask how I was perceiving reality and, when I'm asking the question in that way, I enter the world of *B'ri'ah* and rational psychology or, if you will, humanistic psychology. Finally, I go to the transpersonal, the world of *Atzilut*, which has to do with soul. This means not only the personal subconscious, but a holy unconscious which has archetypes inside, that has God reaching into us. These are very important parts and necessary for completing this process.

When we develop a new practice or custom, the practice has to reflect what happens on the higher levels as well as what happens on the lower level. Some things come from earth, what we can call the chthonic *mitzvot*. For example, I'm sure that we didn't learn how to use compost as a revelation from heaven but rather from being in tune with the earth. Therefore, *mitzvot* which function primarily on this level need to have an earthy quality to them. At the same time, they still need to be connected to heaven, because each *mitzvah* is a fractal containing the gestalt as well as being what it is specifically. The chthonic *mitzvot*, in addition to their earthy gestalt, also have their feeling, reason, and spiritual or moral gestalts. All these have to be like holons one top of one another or like boxes placed one inside the other. So a good *mitzvah* has the organicity of all the forms in it, which lead to the right *kavvanah*. That is the vertical dimension where we deal with God.

There is another vertical dimension to *mitzvot* which connects with all of Israel, past and future. We have to be able to say that our ancestors did this – "*V-hi she-amdah la-avoteinu v-lanu* / This is what stood for our ancestors and for us;" "*Matzah zu she'anu ochlim* / This *matzah* which we eat is the same as the *matzah* our parents ate." There is a level of historic growth which needs to be part of how we develop new or changed practices.

But there is also a horizontal dimension that needs to be considered. A Jew cannot claim that what s/he is doing is fully Jewish if other Jews don't agree that it is Jewish. It's like the son who bought himself a boat with an outboard motor and a captain's cap who told his mother that he was now a captain. She said, "By me you're always a captain, but by captains are you a captain?" That is to say, do other Jews recognize that this is a way to be a Jew?

The horizontal dimension is further complicated, however, by the factor of which groups we mean to include. Most people want to cut off others from their continuum. They want to recognize as good Jews only the people in their narrow range and so, no matter how hard we try, they will not consider what we do to be fully Jewish. However, if we function in an organismic understanding of what *klal yisrael* is, then the practice we develop takes the entire Jewish people into consideration, from the humanistic and secular to the *N'turei Karta* – all of us are one people, organically connected.[25] What this means for me is that the specifics of our *halachah* need to be framed within a larger, universal field which can include many different kinds of people, including those who still live within the older paradigm. The *kashrut* of Jewish specificity, for example, exists within the larger frame of eco-*kashrut*.

---

[25] Literally, the "guardians of the city." This is a group of Jerusalem Jews who oppose Zionism and are considered the most zealous in the Orthodox world.

Practical Considerations for Integral Halachah

Returning to the question of work on *Shabbat*, we have to understand what things we do which we would not delegate to another. For instance, a person who loves gardening as a meditative and stress reducing activity doesn't want to hire a gardener. No person would think to hire someone to make love with his or her spouse! A person who wants to make pots, not in order to sell them, but because s/he loves what happens when centering on the wheel and shaping the clay, will insist on doing this him/herself. Therefore, these activities when done for these reasons may be *shabbosdik* / fully **appropriate to** *Shabbat*.

Most people don't make pots because they have to have them – those they buy. But many people love the artistic outlet pottery provides as a complement to their weekday, professional lives. Rembrandt was commissioned to paint and that is how he made his living. It is very different when a person says that I love to watercolor, but I don't have time to paint all week and only can do it on *Shabbat*. What should we say to them? Is this something that should be permitted on *Shabbat* or not? It's not work that s/he wants to delegate to another and it's not the product which is motivating them, but the effect of the activity itself on their souls. This is the way we need to raise the question when we think about *halachah* for our time.

Then, especially when we are thinking about *Shabbat* and other sacred days, there is the question of timing. I would like to see us continue the ancient practice of lighting candles before sunset on *Shabbat* and holy days. I think it's really important to continue having the awareness that we light candles when dusk comes. On the assumption that we have worked up to the last minute to prepare for *Shabbat* or the holy day, then lighting the candles at dusk is like allowing that energy to propel us into sacred time and carry us higher.

But what happens when we can't do that? Most of us living in the northern and southern hemispheres where there is less daylight in the winter, also live lives governed by the clock rather than the sun. In the winter, it's hard to get home early enough on a Friday to be ready for *Shabbat* at dusk. According to the *halachah* of the previous paradigm, there is no alternative but to say that it's too late to light candles. At the same time, we no longer need candlelight in order to see at night. Rather, candles and incense are the last connections we have to sacrifices on the altar. So it seems appropriate to consider whether we need to soften that insistence on the "correct" candle lighting time so that families don't drive each other crazy because of the clock. Remember that one important reason for lighting candles is *shalom bayit*. What's the point of setting up conflict situations where one family member will be angry at another for running one extra errand on Friday afternoon?

At one time, we were clear that we wanted our prayer to be in Hebrew. The angels, who have to take our prayers to God, know Hebrew best and will garble prayers in other languages and we need their help most when we are not with a *minyan*. It sounds so funny – yet there are certain files that are hard to send from one internet provider to another; they come out as gibberish at the other end. So prayers should be said in Hebrew even if one doesn't understand what s/he is saying, because the angels can deal with Hebrew. There is a Yiddish expression for this rabbinic principle, "*Di malochim fershtein nish kein targum loshen* / The angles don't understand Aramaic!"

Today I feel the opposite. When I come to *shul* I want to *davven* mostly in Hebrew, because that is what Solomon Schechter, the founder of Conservative Judaism, called being part of Catholic Israel. What that means here is that Hebrew is common to us all. A Yemenite or Moroccan Jew can come into an Ashkenazic service and, if the *davvenen* is in Hebrew, can figure out where in the service the congregation is (once s/he masters the differences in pronunciation). So Hebrew is an important element to keep. But when a person *davvens* on his/ her own at home in Hebrew and is rushing through prayers without understanding them, that doesn't make sense.

This is the reverse of the way in which this question was resolved in the previous paradigm. Then the ruling was that it is better to pray in Hebrew when one is alone, because then you need the help of the angels. In public, one can pray in any language because the *Sh'chinnah* is present when there is a *minyan* and therefore the angels aren't needed. That was the old understanding. The new understanding is, psychologically for you, when you're alone, the vernacular is a better way of *davvenen*. I want to say that the simple Jew in North and South America today needs the vernacular and that using it is very helpful.

Teaching for the Hour

There is another principle in *halachah* called *hora'at sha'ah* / teaching of the hour and for the needs of the hour.[26] An example is the famous story of Elijah and the prophets of Ba'al. Since there was a temple in Jerusalem, it was already forbidden to bring sacrifices to any other place. The Torah explicitly states that sacrifices must be brought, *"Ba-makom asher yivchar ha-shem eloheichem bo l-shaken sh'mo sham /* to the place God has chosen to cause the Name to indwell. S*hama tavi'u /* Only there shall you bring everything I command you."[27] Yet, when Elijah wanted to discredit the prophets of the Ba'al, they all set up altars near Mt. Carmel. He asked them to prepare a

---

[26] See, for example, Talmud *Bavli Yoma* 69b. Usually, this means a temporary ruling to deal with a particular situation. However, if a *hora'at sha'ah* becomes accepted practice, it can be become permanent. (ds)

[27] Deuteronomy 12:11.

sacrifice to Ba'al and put it on their altar, but not to light any fire. He did the same and said, "Let's see which God can send a fire down to consume the sacrifice. They start to pray, they gash their bodies, they plead and cry to Ba'al to answer them. Elijah taunts them by saying that maybe Ba'al is asleep and they should cry louder! The whole morning goes by and nothing happens. When it is Elijah's turn, he builds his altar and soaks it with water. Then he prays to God quietly and fire comes down and eats up the sacrifice and the altar and the water.[28] Technically, Elijah should not have done this because he was sacrificing outside the temple, but it was a necessary thing to do at that hour. That's called *hora'at sha'ah*.

The question is, "Are we not today to listen for the teaching of the hour?" When I speak of eco-*kashrut*, that is definitely a teaching of the hour. When we talk about recognizing women in a *minyan* and leading *davvenen*, that too is part of the teaching of the hour. These are the issues these hours have brought to us.

Eco-Kashrut and Ecumenical Considerations

With eco-*kashrut*, our integral *halachah* has to emerge from a gaian consciousness. This is becoming very clear, as we watch how different kinds of people from different world views are becoming aware. Many Evangelical Christians, whose theology I believed would prevent them from acting from a global consciousness, are getting it. This raises ecumenical concerns about how we Jews relate with people of other religions.

As I know I've said in other places, I once tried to get a job in Israel with the *Misrad ha-Datot*, the Religious Ministry. I wanted to be a liaison to other faith communities, to bring a basket of special things to the archimandrite of the Greek Orthodox church and to have a good *shmu'ess* / conversation

---

[28] First Kings 18.

with him. What I wanted was for Jews to relate to other religious leaders in a way that made them feel respected by us. It didn't happen for me and this is not the direction in which things have gone in Israel in relation to other religions. Nevertheless, these inter-faith concerns are still real, namely how we relate with people who belong to other communities in ways which are not insulting to them and where we are not appropriating parts of who they are. Both sides of this are important.

Then there is the principle of *tza'ar ba'alei cha'yim* / **the suffering of living beings.** It is very important to take the suffering of animals into consideration when we talk about *kashrut* in our time.. Recently, very upsetting stories have come out about the slaughterhouse in Iowa. It's supposed to be one of the best as far as *glatt kosher* is concerned and at the same time, animals aren't treated humanely. I know that there are people who have designed ways of holding the animals so they are not freaked out and can expire in a way that holds them rather than by shackling them and pulling them up by their hind legs. So I would like there to be a *kashrut* certificate that says that *tza'ar ba'alei cha'yim* has been observed as well as the laws of *sh'chitah*. This would be like the line we see in movies that says that no animal was hurt in this process.

Reaching In

Another place where an integral *halachah* can be helpful for this moment in time is in dealing with the faith needs of our own communities. I have the feeling that the Jewish federations and the United Jewish Communities, all of which are made up of good, well meaning people, still do not relate well to the faith needs of the community. Even our religious schools don't really know how to relate to these needs, though some of them are beginning to try, bringing in the parents as well so that they can understand what their children are learning. This will help reduce the friction between the schools and the families of the children.

Our social fibers are short and we have to create better support fields. One question for the development of anything in integral *halachah* is, "Does it make for community support or does it weaken it?" Another important rabbinic principle to keep in mind when we think halachically today is, "*Lo nitnu ha-mitzvot ella l-tzaref ba'hem et habri'ot* / The mitzvot were given to connect people to each other."[29] *L'tzaref* can also mean "to put through a crucible, to refine them." Again, both of these things are necessary.

What I mean when I say that we need to pay more attention to the faith needs of our community is that we need to aim for transformation to higher ethical and faith levels. Without going into great detail here, I would mention Lawrence Kohlberg who spoke about moral development and how one goes from one level of moral development to another. In turn, he had a student named James Fowler who talked specifically about faith development. Carol Gilligan, who deals with the same issue, noted that Kohlberg was right but missed women's growth of moral and ethical development. Thus, our conversations about *mitzvah* need a spiritual direction as a core requirement.[30]

For example, at the Passover seder we ask why we eat *matzah?* The answer is to remember that we were slaves and so we shouldn't treat other people the way we were treated by the Egyptians. Another example is the way the rabbis understood the four species that we take in our hands during *Sukkot*. Some people are full of *mitzvot*, here meaning good deeds, and full of Torah, meaning learning. They are like the *etrog* / citron, which

---

[29] Midrash *B'reishit Rabbah* 44:1.

[30] See "*Shi'ur* One: Introduction" in the next section of this book.

has both a good smell and a good taste. (Torah is the taste, m*itzvo*t is the smell.) Then there are those who are like the *hadassim* / **myrtle leaves**, which have a good smell but no taste. These people are full of *mitzvot*, but without much learning. Then there are those who are like the *lulav* / **palm branch**. Because this is from a date palm, it has a taste but no smell. People who are like the palm have learning, but lack the fragrance of those who are full of *mitzvot*. Then there are the *aravot* / **willow leaves**, that have neither taste nor smell. These people are neither learned nor full of *mitzvot*. Nevertheless, it the foursome that is held together, with all that can be learned from that. Each *mitzvah* has to have a component that somehow brings out a meaning for us, and you can see how we made that true in the past from these examples.

When looked at in this way, a "good" *mitzvah* reduces our resistance to God. Let me give another example. There is a rule on Purim that *kol ha-poshet yado li-tol notnim lo* / **you have to give to anyone who extends a hand.**[31] In Europe, the custom was that people who didn't need the *tz'dakah* themselves were the ones who collected *tz'dakah* for others. My father, *alav ha-shalom*, did this himself. When he went around collecting *tz'dakah* on Purim, people knew that since it was Reb Shlomo collecting, it certainly was for a good cause, so people gave liberally. In this way, people could also fulfill the *mitzvah* of *tz'dakah* at the highest level that Maimonides listed, namely that neither the giver nor the recipient were known to one another.

Once, a particular man saw him coming and turned quickly to the East and began *davvening shmoneh esrei.*[32] My dad sidled up to him and whispered, "*V-anshei sdom ra'im v-chata'im lashem m'od* / **The people of Sodom were wicked and sinful, but**

---

[31] Rambam *Hilchot M'gillah* 2:16

[32] The 18 Blessings or the *Amidah*, during which time it is forbidden to interrupt oneself or to interrupt another.

they made themselves very holy to God."[33] He was giving this guy a dig and hinting that he would come back when he had finished with the *shmoneh esrei*! He was not going to let him off the hook and allow him to escape the *mitzvah* of giving. Sometimes people use one *mitzvah* as a pretext for being present, for appearing to offer themselves to God. It is a pretext because they are using it to avoid another *mitzvah* which may be even more important for their relationship with God. What we have to watch out for, then, is to be sure that the way we work with *mitzvot* is always to reduce the resistance to God.

What God Wants From Us

The key here is that God needs something from us. This is something that often doesn't play a prominent role in modern approaches to Judaism. I want to say very clearly that the early reformers didn't have a sense that God needed anything from us. They were in a lineage that went back through Hermann Cohen to Kant, who in turn was in harmony with many other philosophers on this issue. What they said was that God was impassible, that God doesn't need anything from humanity because God is perfect. Then, the middle of the twentieth century, Abraham Joshua Heschel wrote a book called *God in Search of Man*, returning to the older Jewish position that the whole point of creation is that God is in search of a partner in and a relationship with human beings. This is also what the anthropic principle suggests and is reminiscent of Moses' question in the Torah, "*V-atah Yisra'el, mah Hashem Elohecha sho'el mei-imach* / And now, Israel, what does God want from you?"[34] You cannot create a Judaism, much less a *halachah*, without taking that question into consideration.

---

[33] Genesis 13:13. Literally this means that the people of Sodom were very wicked before God. This way of reading the verse places a comma between "wicked and sinful" and "before God." The people of Sodom were wicked and sinful in their lives, but they continued praying to God.

[34] Deuteronomy 10:12.

What is it, then, that God wants from us? First and foremost, it is to create a God-field in the world. Whatever judgments we might make about the people in the religious right and Islamic fundamentalists, for example, what they are trying to do is to make up in an unskillful way for the lack of the God-field in today's world. Unless you watch a channel which is specifically religious, this absence is obvious when you watch TV. The sense that this is not our world, but God's, and that we all have to serve in our different and unique ways, is rarely shown. This is another important concern when we build our integral *halachah*.

Second is a sense of holiness. I mentioned before that walking into many churches brings with it a sense of awe and mystery. While I like the social dimension of going to *shul*, the way we love and talk with one another, I also like it very much when our services begin with half an hour in silence. When that happens, people who come in during the silence walk in quietly and on tiptoe. This is a way of recognizing that this is not my turf but God's place. *"B-veit Elohim n'halech b-ragesh* / **In a house of God we walk on tiptoe**" would be a way of translating these words.[35]

Third is to recognize that we want the *Sh'chinah* to dwell with us. When I was a little kid, my Papa, *alav ha-shalom*, would put on his *tallis* and wrap it around himself and over his head. I liked to creep under the *tallis* and be with Papa. In my way at that time, I wanted to be *tachat kanfei ha-Sh'chinah* / **under the wings of the *Sh'chinah***. I wanted to really feel the Divine Presence, that sense of the feminine. *Torat imecha* / **The mother's Torah**, has to be there.

Fourth is *d'vekut*, "nearer my God to Thee." After I've done a *mitzvah*, do I feel closer to God or not? In traditional language, this is called becoming a *merkavah* / **vehicle** for doing

---

[35] Psalm 55:15.

God's work. But there are two ways to understand this. In the disagreements between Hillel and Shammai, one approach is that we follow Hillel because he is more lenient and his way is more accessible. However, the Talmud says that the words of both are the words of the living God. If that is true, then what is the value of Shammai's approach? So the second approach says that we follow Hillel as a kind of compromise, since we are not yet ready to live this *mitzvah* at its deepest level. When *Mashi'ach* comes, then we will be able to follow Shammai.

What this is really trying to say is that most of the *mitzvot* that we've done until now are a compromise between what God wants and what we can afford to do. But if we want to change the texture of life on the planet, we need to begin to live Messianic *halachah* now. Rabbi Arthur Waskow was so right when he took the expression *hilchata li-m'shicha* / the law when Mashi'ach will come and read it as the law which takes us toward *Mashi'ach*;[36] this is a law that will bring us closer to *Mashi'ach*. In other words, instead of waiting for *Mashi'ach*, how would you behave now if *Mashi'ach* had already come? It's similar to when Christian fundamentalists ask, "What would Jesus do?" or "What kind of car would Jesus drive?"

The Consensus of the Committed

Integral *Halachah* is not mine to define forever. At best I can give some guidelines now for others to work with. When people ask me why other people in Renewal don't do things like I do, my answer is that we are a microcosm of *k'lal yisra'el*, we are an organism. The heart does something different than the liver and so each of us has our part to do. When people cite Maimonides or the *Shulchan Aruch* -- which really means that this is how Reb Yosef Karo laid it down – or the *Chofetz Chayim* in the *Mishnah B'rurah*, they are saying that this is how

---

[36] Talmud *Bavli Sanhedrin* 51b.

everybody should do things. On the other hand, we say go out and see what people are actually doing, like I said about American kosher. What is the consensus of the committed today?

I like to speak of the consensus of the committed, because we rely on the committed for an upward striving and a desire for transformation. When they manifest a consensus, it is one we can count on. Those who say, like the man my father approached, "Leave me alone. I have fulfilled my obligation and extricated myself from the grasp of my duty. I've done the minimum and I'm done," cannot shape what Integral Halachah will become. The way they do things doesn't do anything for the psyche; it only satisfies some of the outer behavioral forms of *halachah*.

So we are not talking about user friendly corner cutting, we are not talking about Judaism lite. The process of creating the structure of Integral Halachah will take time. It will take more of the consensus of the pious, with more input from women, and we'll make more mistakes. Buckminster Fuller pointed this out when he said that biologically, organically, we are made in such a way that we can't learn except when we make a mistake.

The *G'mara* says the same thing. "*Ein adam omed al divrei Torah ella im ken nichshal bahen /* No person can really get straight about the words of Torah unless s/he has stumbled first."[37] Only when you see why it doesn't pay to do it that way, do you discover the other way which works better. I'll give you an example that goes back to the seventies. A couple named Nena and George O'neill wrote a book called *Open Marriage*. Later, she changed her mind and wrote in favor of marital fidelity in another book called *The Marriage Premise*. What happened? *Nichshal bahen*, there was too much bad karma created, so she learned from that. In the same way, we have learned that

---

[37] Talmud *Bavli Gittin* 43a.

cutting down the challenge of *Yiddishkeit*, saying that we want to lower the standards, hasn't worked for us. Without a conscious commitment to growth in the direction of more transformation, *Yiddishkeit* can't continue.

No one learns without making mistakes. The only thing we can give each other is a *brachah* that the mistakes from which we learn should be small ones and the consequences should not be dire. *Y'hi ratzon* that we should all embody the way of Integral Halachah, *v'nomar*

Amen.

PART TWO
SHI'UR ONE: ELEMENTS OF INTEGRAL HALACHAH

Introduction

A Kavvanah / Intention

Baruch atah YAH Eloheinu chei ha-olamim, asher kid'shanu b-mitzvotav v-tzivanu al divrei Torah. V-ha'arev na, YAH Eloheinu, et divrei torat'cha b-finu, u-v-fi chol am'cha beit yisrael. V-ni'hi'ye anachnu, v-tze'e'tza'einu, v-tze'e'tza'ei tze'e'tza'einu, v-tze'e'tza'einu ad sheva dorot v-ad olam, kulanu yod'ei sh'mecha v-lomdei torat'cha li-sh'mah. Baruch atah YAH, ha-m'lameid Torah l-amo yisra'el. Amein.

Praised are You, *YAH* our God, life of the worlds, who has made us holy through *mitzvot* and commanded us about words of Torah. *YAH* our God, make the words of your Torah pleasant in our mouths and in the mouths of all your people, the house of Israel. May we and our children, and the children of our children, and our descendants seven generations in the future and forever, all be among those who know your Name and learn your Torah for *Sh'chinah*'s sake. Praises to you, *YAH*, who teaches Torah to the people Israel. Amen.[1]

Before beginning to discuss specific issues in *halachah*, I want to provide a context. It is important for us to understand the larger forces which shaped our practice in the past and to clarify where I think we are now. What we call *halachah* is largely about the specifics of behavior and, in the ongoing

---

[1] This blessing has more than one form. Here, Reb Zalman is following most closely that form found in the *siddur* of *Chabad*, the *Chassidic* school from which he comes. In addition, Reb Zalman has modified the traditional form to say "for seven generations" and beyond, in the way that many Native Americans speak.

effort to clarify details, it is easy to lose the connection between the minutiae of practice and the spiritual vision from which they are derived. Then, I will use the four part division of the *Shulchan Aruch,* choosing specific issues and discussing them in reference to these larger forces.

A Modern Midrash

Let me begin with a modern *midrash* using the three ways we are commanded to love God in the verse which immediately follows the *sh'ma yisra'el*; namely that we are to love God *b-chol l'vav'cha* / with all your heart, *u-v-chol naf'sh'cha* / with all your soul, *u-v-chol m'odecha* / with all your strength.[2]

B-chol l'vav'cha was the time of the *Beit HaMikdash* / Holy Temple, during the age of Aries, when clarifying dualities was the primary issue. In a way, this is what the medieval Biblical commentator *Rashi*[3] was seeing when he interpreted this expression as meaning *b-shnei yitzarecha* / with your two inclinations, the *yeitzer ha-ra* / inclination toward evil and the *yeitzer ha-tov* / inclination toward good. Looking back at the biblical age, the rabbis were trying to say that people are pulled in two directions and each of those directions has the potential for sanctity. One the one hand, people were pulled toward the worship of *Ba'al* and *Asherah* and their temples. On the other, people were pulled toward YHVH and the sanctuary in Jerusalem. To serve the Infinite, one needed to find ways to combine both tendencies.

U-v-chol naf'sh'cha was the time of exile. First, there was the exile which lasted for seventy years following the destruction of the *Beit HaMikdash* in 586 BCE. Then, in the

---

[2] Deuteronomy 6:5.

[3] *Rashi* is an acronym for Rabbeinu Shlomo Yitzchaki, our teacher Solomon the son of Isaac (1040-1105). He, in turn, is citing an earlier rabbinic *midrash* (*Sifri V-etchanan piska* 7).

year 70 CE, the second temple was destroyed and we entered
into the age of Pisces. When commenting on the words, *b-chol
naf'sh'cha*, *Rashi* says: *"Afilu hu notayl et naf'sh'cha* / [Love God]
even if He takes your life." I think of all the sacrifices made by
the Jewish people during the age of Pisces, all the human
sacrifices, from Rabbi Akiva and the others known as the *asarah
harugei malchut* / ten murdered by the [Roman] government
through all the generations, the massacres which continued all
the way to our own time, to Auschwitz. This was an age of
loving God *b-chol naf'sh'cha*.

Now I believe that we are coming to the time of *b-chol
m'odecha*. If, in the age of Aries, the concern was with bringing
dualities into harmonious relationship with one another and, in
the age of Pisces, with the need to sacrifice the individual to the
transcendent, then this is the time of the merging of the
immanent within the world with the transcendent beyond. The
Hebrew *m'od* can mean "all that one has." It can also mean
with every quality of one's being or with all one's strength; a
pushing beyond normal limits. It is identification with that level
of the soul called *y'chidah* / unified or singular; that level most
connected to the infinite source.[4] It is the merging of the
individual perspective with the collective to reduce the strain
humanity places on the planet and to become more aware of
the interdependence of its bio-systems. This is the age and level
hinted in the *midrash* which says, commenting on the words
"'God is One:' Let the soul which is unique in the body come
and praise God who is unique in the world."[5]

Now the question is, "What is the *avodah* / mode of service
of *b-chol m'odecha*, with the *y'chidah* level of the soul? This is what
is called *avodah b-m'sirut ha-nefesh* in various sources. It means

---

[4] A hint of this meaning of soul can be found in the *Tosafot*, Talmud *Bavli
M'nachot* 18a (עד לאחת).

[5] Leviticus *Rabbah* (Margaliot) 4:8.

that something is happening in which the ego gets set aside, in which it is surrendered to something larger. I think of *m'sirut nefesh* as ego surrender.

Paradigm Shift

Realizing that we are talking about service and practice at this level makes us aware that we are doing something new, something we are being called to do in order to renew Judaism's connection to the Divine call which sits at its core. At the same time, whenever I say that what we're doing is new, people respond by asking, "But didn't those who came before also say that what they were doing was new? Why do you insist on claiming that we are living in a time of paradigm shift? Isn't it really the same in every generation?"

My response is that what we are doing now is not the same as the process of change as it manifests in most generations. There are some essential differences that make what is happening a true shift in paradigm. And, just as we had to learn how to get along without a *Beit HaMikdash* and to reformat Judaism accordingly, so we now have to reformat Judaism again to this totally different way of doing things.

Let me give you an illustration of how difficult it is to resolve our questions using only the rules which worked in the previous paradigm. There is a book of responsa written by an Orthodox rabbi whom we call the *M'lamed l-Ho'il* after the name of his book and who lived between the two world wars.[6] He was a wonderful rabbi who was trying to respond to the difficult questions people were asking him, questions which his forbears had not been asked. People asked him about intermarriages, about children born from common-law unions which had not been formalized under a *chuppah* / wedding

---

[6] Rabbi David Tzvi Hoffman was born in Verbo, Hungary, in 1843, and died in Berlin in 1921.

canopy and with *kiddushin* / a formal contract of betrothal, about how to make a *mikveh* using city water, and about how to translate the measurements of the Talmud into centimeters. He talked about whether using electricity is like lighting a fire and other modern issues.

Nevertheless, he discussed these issues in the halachic language that he had inherited and which was really inadequate to his task. For example, can one truly answer the question of whether one can use a thermos bottle on *shabbos* using only the traditional categories of *eirrui* and *bishul*.[7] He was wonderful in his willingness to face these issues. The range of his knowledge was phenomenal and it was equaled by his concern for people. He often said that the only reason he responded to these questions was because he understood the situations in which people found themselves. At the same time, I think he realized the limitations which the traditional halachic system placed on him and that he would rather have not functioned in this capacity.

The truth is that it is the chessboard itself that is changing. However much we might desire to live according to the *p'sakim* / rulings of the *M'lamed l-Ho'il*, it really is not possible. We are moving toward an altogether, different place, one where we have to make radical choices and shifts. We can neither ignore these shifts nor shirk the immense responsibility which accompanies them.

Some Implications of Paradigm Shift

When I say that this is a time of paradigm shift, we now actually have an image for it which makes the impact on our thoughts and awareness graphically visible. I'm referring to being able to see our planet from outer space. These well

---

[7] The issue is whether pouring water from a thermos over food is *eirrui* / transfusion and *bishul* / cooking.

known photographs are a symbol that we see over and over again that touches our hearts and has such a powerful impact on us. They give us a new way to understand the phrase *melech ha-olam* / ruler of the world, which is central to every blessing we recite; God as the *melech* of that *olam* seen from outer space.

In a profound way, this image of the Earth as seen from space makes God more accessible, not less. Scientific research and cosmological theories have made the universe ever bigger and, to the cosmic Infinite, I'm not even a flea on the back of a flea. However, to see myself as a brain-cell of mother earth is a privilege; to live and have this connection to the planet. From the notion of a God who creates and sustains the life of the planet there emerges an organic understanding of our world, which is different from a hierarchical understanding. Now, when we talk about *olam*, we are talking about the larger organism of whom we are a part, whom we love and for whom we care, and who needs us in order to heal.

That, in turn, means that there has to be a *m'sirat nefesh*, a taking of that which is in ego, giving it away and saying, "The larger whole is what's important now." If I were to reframe this in a traditional expression, I would say, "*Harei ani moser et nafshi, ruchi, v-nishmati l-nefesh, ru'ach, n'shama shel kaddur ha-aretz* / I give myself away, I want my *m'sirat ha-nefesh* to be not seeking my own ends, but to seek what will help the purpose of the planet" and add to its healing. This is a paradigm shift at a level we haven't seen in any previous generation.

For so long, the most important thing for Jews was to maintain the integrity of our ethnicity, to stay together, and to overcome ethnic adversaries. Now we see that putting the interests of our ethnicity first has become bankrupt and is an approach that can no longer be sustained. This is so clear when when I look at what happened in the Balkans and also how we find a solution to the conflict between Israelis and Palestinians.

So, my sense is that we have arrived at an unprecedented place.

Of The Mind / The "Integral" of Integral Halachah

In order, then, to be able to do the work required by the paradigm shift in which we are living, we have to reformat our brains and begin to use more of our brain capacity. Today, if a person uses 10% of their brain, *mah tov u-mah na'im* / how wonderful that is. But this is no longer enough. We have been able to reach our current technological level using that small percentage of our total brain capacity, and this is truly amazing. However, we are not yet smart enough to do this without injuring the earth. To accomplish this, we need to become smarter. While we are very smart when it comes to building ways of destruction and death, we haven't yet become as smart in the issues of peace.

Imagine if you will a scene from Star Trek. In order to solve the next set of problems, I need to use all the memory available to both Data and the ship's computer. When I ask Chief O'Brian whether the computers have more memory, he responds by saying that 80% of the potential memory is still unused. However, it is not available right away because it has yet to be formatted. And, unless we find a way to format that potential memory, we won't able to solve the next set of problems.

Now we can begin to understand why the psychological aspect of Integral Halachah is so important. It is not only that we need to handle the problems that we have; we also have to handle the internal machinery of the mind with which we are going to solve these problems. Continuing the computer analogy, we have go into the system files of the head and restructure consciousness itself.

Klal Yisra'el and Jewish Renewal

While we are engaged in this universal work, we also need to create a Judaism which is renewed and living, which allows people with expanded consciousness to stay Jewish. We all know that there are people who have had many wonderful insights, epiphanies, and then have difficulties integrating with a *minyan*. The epiphanies may have come from Buddhism; they may have come from psychedelic drugs; they may have come from meditation; or they may have come from being in nature. Whatever the source, the insights and epiphanies are real. What followed is the realization that what goes on in the average synagogue is kindergarten in comparison to these epiphanies.

That is what this *shi'ur* is all about; to start thinking about the kind of *Yiddishkeit* we have to create, the kind of *Yiddishkeit* for which we have to prepare. And this gives us the responsibility which I mentioned earlier.

One thing that happens when people decide to work at this level where they are changing the system files of Judaism, as it were, making adjustments to the basic structure, is that it makes others uncomfortable. They worry about the integrity of these files, believing them to sit so close to the core that they must always remain the same. Some may publicly and vociferously challenge the credentials of those who work at this deep level. They also raise the legitimate concern that changing the core can make things worse.

Now we find ourselves in a second tension: The first level of tension requires that we renew Judaism in a way which is both universal and authentic to Jewish particularity. The second level requires that we work so close to the core that we arouse fear and resistance from the very people whose Jewish particularity we need to validate. If we don't get into the core files of Judaism, then we believe that we can't survive. At the same time, if do get into the core and make mistakes in this unprecedented work, then we also can't survive.

So we have to meditate deeply and engage in serious study and prayer before entering these system files to make the changes and adjustments that are necessary. We have to be careful in what we do and propose so that our work doesn't create more *tzoris* / problems than we are trying to solve. We have to balance universal truths with the principle of keeping *k'lal yisra'el* / the totality of Israel together, since *k'lal yisra'el* may very well be an enzyme that the earth needs in order to live. If the earth is a living and conscious entity, then Judaism and the Jewish people can be seen as one of that body's vital organs. For the same reasons that we worry about the effect on the ecology of the planet of the loss of species diversity, so we need to be concerned about the loss of individual religions and spiritual practices, including our own, and the effect of these losses on the overall health of the earth's consciousness.

This is the amazing task that we have taken on, a task which calls for *m'sirat nefesh* as much as it calls for a kind of holy *chutzpah*.

Halachic Anchors

When the starting place is an epiphany, it leads to a willingness to attempt such fundamental reformatting. When the reformatting appears successful, then what happens is that everything seems to have become relative.

This, in turn, leads to the idea which appears widespread both within the movement for Jewish spiritual renewal and to those who look in from the outside, that in Jewish renewal you can do anything as long as it feels right. This comes from the desire we have to go back to nature, to the origin places of our practices. Judaism seems to have become something only of the mind; something to be learned primarily from books. We wanted to rediscover the primary experiences which gave rise to the traditions, to feel Judaism in our *kishkes* / guts, to have Judaism inform our daily lives and feelings. And this desire is correct. Yet, as much as we need our messages to come from the direct experience of the Divine Presence within us, from how we are in our bodies, at the same time we also need to have a sense of what is absolute in our lives, which is equally essential and decisive. When everything becomes relative and negotiable, then we can't really talk about Torah or *halachah* anymore. Without Torah and *halachah*, we no longer have Judaism.

We have, therefore, arrived at the central question of this book, which is about *halachah*. And that question is, "Where in the Judaism we are renewing can we anchor an approach to *halachah*?"

Autonomous "Anchors"

In the past, if we were to ask this same question, "Where did you anchor *halachah*?," the answer was that we anchored *halachah* in what is called *heteronomy*, in something outside ourselves. "God, who lives in the heavens, descended onto Mt. Sinai and gave us the Torah. From then on, it has been our obligation to live up to its expectations of us."

For so many centuries, then, our refrain was, *"M'loch al kol ha-olam kulo bi-ch'vodechah* / [God], reign over the whole world in your glory!"[8] Now, as we experience ourselves within this paradigm shift, we have begun also to say something like, "God, enter into this world and become manifest in our lives." For us, God has become primarily immanent. We look less for God on the outside and more on the inside.

---

[8] This is the opening line of the conclusion of the *malchuyot* / sovereignty section of the *musaf* / additional prayer on *Rosh HaShannah*.

However, when our experience of God is on the inside and therefore more subjective, how can we distinguish between that which is idiosyncratic to me and that which comes from God? These teachings were originally prepared for the ALEPH Kallah whose theme was "Growing Souls, Growing Community," where we were not only dealing with individual souls but also with building community. Somehow, we need to work together to build the linkages between individual experiences of the Divine on the inside and shared community on the outside.

Consensus of the Pious

I believe that there is a field into which we can anchor a viable approach to *halachah* which I call our "shared consensus," a modern version of the traditional principle called the "consensus of the pious."

The question then becomes, "How do we define piety in Jewish Renewal?" In the older system, where Torah was seen as coming from the outside, the definition could be largely quantifiable. It was based on attention to detail in practice and a measurable depth and breadth of learning. For us, I think it needs to have an added, and central, ingredient which is about *kavvanah* / intention and attitude. It's the way in which one says, "Good *Shabbos*," the way in which one gives a *brochah* / blessing to another, the way in which one makes *freilach* / experiences joy on *Shabbos*, the way in which one *davvens* / prays. It also involves the way in which a leader focuses on empowering others rather than using his/her knowledge to maintain a place at the top of a hierarchy. It is in the way in which prayer services can happen in a circle and skills are shared. What I am trying to say is that the pious of our time are identified by the way in which they bring Jewish spiritual practice out into the world; how they make it come alive.

At the same time, it is not enough to say that the consensus of those who have the appropriate *kavvanah* is sufficient. We also have to anchor our *halachah* in common practice. For example, there is a *halachic k'lal* / general principle that goes like this: The residents of one town made an agreement that, in order to support the local *shochet* / ritual slaughterer, they would recognize only this one person's *sh'chitah* / slaughter. Any meat which was slaughtered outside that town and then brought it would be considered *treifa* / not kosher.[9]

This is not an ontological statement. It may very well have been that the *shochet* in the next town was more *frumm*, a more expert *shochet*. Nevertheless, our group has the right to declare something forbidden only for them. And, once that thing is declared forbidden, it becomes an absolute anchor.[10]

So what I want to say is that we need to begin work on uncovering what our consensus is. I don't think that we know enough yet to establish this consensus; it's too early in this process. But I do think we can begin conversations now which will lead to this consensus, so that when we gather at our *kallot* and conferences in the near future we might be able to identify some of the absolutes, non-negotiables, and boundaries. This is the way we will program our immune system, so that we will be able to agree that, "If these boundaries aren't kept, Judaism falls apart."

A Jewish "Immune System"

All over the world, people are dealing with the issue of AIDS. The universality of AIDS points to a deficiency in the auto-immune system of the human race. On the spiritual level, the fact that 52% of born-Jews are not affiliated with their

[9] See *Shulchan Aruch Yoreh De'ah* 1:11.

[10] Because it falls into the general principle of *takkanat ha-kahal*, a ruling made by the community to which all members of that community become obligated (Ibid. 228:33).

people and may be fading away,[11] points to a deficiency in the auto-immune system of Judaism which, if healthy, would act to keep them Jewishly identifiable. Since I believe that it is necessary for there to be Jews in the world, I take this deficiency seriously.

Thus, the issue of anchoring is crucial to resolve. We need to know what the consensus of our pious is, we need to know how to identify those whom we would call pious, we need to see what common practice is, and we have to reach out and include as many people as we can. On the one hand, we need absolutes and, on the other, we need to be inclusive. How are we going to go about doing this?

Anchors That Align

A crucial element of *halachahic* practice is feeling that we are aligning ourselves with God's will. This does not require that we think of God as coming from the outside; it can be the God from the inside – but it is still something we do because God wants us to. Things that fit into this category can become our absolutes.

To begin the discussion which leads to a clearer sense of what our consensus might become, I want to suggest three principles which I see as directly supporting aligning with the Divine will and within which the specifics of our consensus might fall. These follow the traditional halachic examples of the three primary absolutes, those *mitzvot* for which a person should *yei'hareg v-al ya'avor* / be killed rather than violate.[12]

---

[11] For a recent and careful analysis and evaluation of the current data on Jewish involvement, please see "A Tale of Two Jewries: The 'Inconvenient Truth' for American Jews" by Steven M. Cohen (2006; Jewish Life Network/Steinhardt Foundation and Steven Cohen).

[12] See *Sanhedrin* 74a.

Sustainable Ecology

The first of the traditional absolutes is the ban on *avodah zarah* / worshipping false gods in public. I would extend the concept of idolatry to include the issue of toxic things and pollution. The first great absolute I see today is, "To injure Earth is *yei'hareg v-al ya'avor*, one should rather die than violate this principle and do something which creates or enhances an ecological imbalance, further endangering life on this planet. On this, there is no give.

Thus, if someone were to come and say to me, "Either you poison this river or else I'm going to kill you," I would have to say, "Kill me." I believe that if we don't have an absolute principle around this issue, then we can't claim to have a *halachah* at all. So I submit that *avodah zarah*, today's idolatry, is any practice which risks the *kiyum* / survival of our world.

Sustainable Judaism

The second principle for which a person must be willing to sacrifice his/her own life is that of *gilui arayot*,[13] which is anything that would dissolve a familial unit of *yiddishkeit*. I feel that one needs to be *mosser nefesh* and choose to make the needs of the people more important than the desires of the individual. So the second principle would be formulated as having to do with the *kiyum* of the Jewish entity, or the Jewish organ of the whole planet.

Self Determination

The third principle is that of *sh'fichat damim* / killing another to save one's own life. Today, I think we need to formulate this as, "I cannot do anything that would take away from another human being his/her self-determination."

---

[13] Literally this means the exposure of nakedness and refers to violation of the prohibitions against incest and adultery.

So, we can say that these three traditional principles still express how we can claim to know God's will and, if we can anchor their meaning in a new consensus of the pious, then this becomes God's will for us to the point that anything that doesn't meet this standard is our *treifa*.

Or Ha-T'shuvah

In order to move towards a shared approach to interpreting these principles for our time, we have to also understand the emerging cosmologies and the shift in reality maps in our world. And, going beyond cognition, we need to allow these changes to enter our thinking, our *davvenen,* and our ways of relating to one another. We need to live fully in the awareness that we are part of the living earth and that she uses those of us that can see and hear as her means to change and heal.

The core of our *t'shuvah* / return, is a push for change rather than a return to a previous state. It is an expansion of the traditional concept of *t'shuvah* to include both the individual's physical body and the sense in which the planet can be seen as the body of all living creatures as one.[14] It reminds me of when President Clinton's campaign slogan was, "It's the economy, stupid." To me that becomes, "It's about change, stupid." If we don't understand change, then we won't make it. There is a *midrash* which says that without the ability to change one's behavior, to return, the world could not endure. God's hand is always extended to receive those who return, as it says, "*Shuvu banim shovavim* / Return wayward children."[15] Today, I hear this as meaning that the *bat kol* comes from the belly of the center of the Earth and it's saying "Heal me my children, heal me! And you must do it differently."

---

[14] I am especially grateful here to Seth Fishman for this reading of Reb Zalman's intent. (ds)

[15] This *midrash* appears in several forms. This one is from *Pirkei d'Rabbi Eliezer* 42. The biblical quote is from Jeremiah 3:14 or 22.

When we feel this energy entering our *kishkas*, it is a call for change that Rav Kook identified as the *or ha-t'shuvah* / light of return.[16] All that we do which rides that current will be in the flow of the needed changes. They will help the individual survive and contribute to the healing of the planet. Whatever tries to block this current of change will draw life's antibodies to it, which will seek to either dissolve it or encapsulate it and get rid of it.

Shared Values

Understanding the changes in cosmology and the nature of *t'shuvah* is the first step in approaching a modern definition of our shared values using the three major principles. A second step is to give a name that will express the depth at which these values are shared. In the past, we identified these shared values through the expressions "*Torah mi-sinai* / Torah from Sinai" and "*Halachah l-moshe mi-sinai* / A law given to Moses at Sinai." My sense is that to say something is *halachah l-moshe mi-sinai* was their way of saying, "This is something we have accepted as being the consensus of the pious, the way we do it. It doesn't need any further *p'sukim* / verses used for documentation."

For example, "We've decided that *t'fillin* are going to be black. It is *halachah l-moshe mi-sinai*." "*T'fillin* are going to be cubed; *halachah l-moshe mi-sinai*." To say this is *halachah l-moshe mi-sinai* was a way of saying that this is the consensus of the pious.

When Dennis Prager calls for non-Orthodox commitment, he means that he would like to see a Judaism that has value, that has power, that can help people, that can serve as a guarantor of values, and at the same time is not Orthodox. Mordecai Kaplan used to say that God is the guarantor of our

---

[16] Rabbi Abraham Isaac Kook, first modern Ashkenazi chief rabbi of Israel. He authored a book by this name (*Orot ha-T'shuvah*).

values, and that means that there is something which is absolute, which in turn raises the significance of the shared consensus as our means of hearing the daily call to *t'shuvah* emanating from *Sh'chinah*.[17]

Seven Generations

Third, our understanding of how to approach our core values requires a longitudinal view which extends beyond only this present moment.

The problem with the insights of the (nineteen)sixties was that is was all about the here and now. "Be here now" was the slogan and the title of Ram Dass' famous book. Now, this was a wonderful insight, because it added an important complement to what was a way of doing things focused too much in the head. At that moment, it was important to re-balance with a focus on the "here and now." However, the other expression of the time was, "Don't trust anyone over thirty;" which meant, don't accept anything from the past.

This rejection of the past was wrong, because it meant that we were not thinking in a longitudinal way. We were thinking only about one generation, which more recently led us to ask whether Jewish renewal would be only a one generation phenomenon.

We need to learn to think about things at least, as the native Americans say, "in seven generations." I think about this commitment to a multi-generational thought process every time I say *v-shomru*.[18] "*La-asot et ha-shabbat l-dorotam, b'rit olam* / To make the *Shabbat* in all their generations, an eternal covenant."

---

[17] Kaplan, *The Meaning of God*, p. 29 (cited from http://www.jrf.org/cong/res-recon-God.html).

[18] Exodus 31:16-17, used as part of the *kiddush* on *Shabbat* day as well as in the morning *Amidah* for *Shabbat*. There is also the biblical concept that all our actions reverberate beyond our lifetimes; bad for four generations, good for a a thousand (Exodus 34:6).

It breaks my heart when I think that some of my *kinderlach*[19] might not know from *Shabbos*, and so I want to do everything that I can that they should have *Shabbos*.

At the same time, I don't want them to have a *Shabbos* made up only of prohibitions. I want them to have a *Shabbos* that will be a manifestation of what is good for the planet in seven generations; the kind of *Shabbos* that all people on the planet can share, because it will be the day the Earth heals herself and stops working so that she can return to herself. This what I mean by thinking in a longitudinal way.

I must add that this way of thinking introduces an important caution, particularly when it comes to genetic and bio-engineering. So far, I have been saying that we have an obligation to open up Judaism's system files, in spite of the risks involved. Genetic engineering is also a way of inserting ourselves into the system files of life. I realize that there is potential for healing in this work, but we have also learned that everything we do has a shadow cost. So we must proceed with caution and work to develop the ethics of bio-engineering as part of the process of creating Integral Halachah.[20]

Jewish Mantras: The Sheish Z'chirot

I want you to realize that the shifts I am talking about and the new ways we need to relate to *halachah* should not be attempted light-heartedly. People tend to focus on only the first half of the well-known statement by Rabbi Mordecai Kaplan, namely that the tradition and the past do not have a veto over changes required by the present. That may be true; but he also

---

[19] Literally, "my children." Reb Zalman is referring to his, and our, descendants.

[20] A practical outgrowth of Reb Zalman's thinking was the interfaith Sacred Food Project which ALEPH initiated in 2005.

said that they do have a vote, or a voice as I would say it. It is important for us to really listen to these voices from our past since, by not paying attention to them, we might be tempted to over-steer, which is as dangerous as steering too little.

Not only do these shifts need to be made carefully, they also need to be made consciously. This consciousness will allow us to be aware of the outcomes of our actions, only some of which will have immediate results and feedback. Most of them will take longer; perhaps a single generation or lifetime, or maybe even the seven generations I spoke of earlier. Knowing this obligates us to being tentative, responsible, and conscious, as well as taking the time to deeply understand those practices and beliefs we seek to change.

To help us cultivate this consciousness and carefulness, I suggest becoming familiar with something in traditional *siddurim* / prayer-books, called the *Sheish Z'chirot* / Six Remembrances, the short list of things that you have to remember as a daily practice.[21] These include, *Yom asher amad'ta lifney ha-shem elokecha b-chorev* / The day you stood before YHVH your God at *Choreiv* (Sinai), going out of Egypt, *Shabbat*, Miriam. Remember. These are the things you have to keep inside yourself and always available, like memory-resident programs which say, "If you keep these things memory-resident, then you will be able to do the right work."

Mental Mitzvot

The things we have to remember lead me to the question-of where do we keep our awareness? In order to work on ourselves and to keep in mind those things we need to remember, there are the *mitzvot ha-t'luyot ba-lev* / *mitzvot* that are heart (thought and intention) dependent. Reb Ahrele Roth's 32 *mitzvot* that one

---

[21] The reader can also find the *Sheish Z'chirot* in the booklet called *Yom Kippur Kattan and Cycles of T'shuvah*, available from the ALEPH ReSources Catalog.

can fulfill as *chovot ha-l'vavot* / **obligations of the heart**, are really important in this work. These are *mitzvot* that one strives to do continually in-every moment.[22]

I remember-that years ago I would give my friends a little bell to hang in their cars to help in this practice. The bell would ring whenever the car hit a pothole or a bump. I called it a "*Nu*-bell," since whenever the bell rang, it was saying, "*Nu?*" It reminded them to focus on one of these *mitzvot* which are heart-dependent: "Aha!

- I love You God.

- You are One.

- I respect You.

- I place my faith and my trust in You.

- I ask You to help me live a good life."

I would say to the people to whom I gave these bells that if, *chalilah v-chas* / **God forbid**, I have to die in an automobile accident, then the last thing I would hear is the bell. Then, instead of going out saying, "Oh sh..", I would go out saying something like, "*Echad, yachid u-m'yuchad* / **One, singular, and unique** (is God)."

These heart-dependent *mitzvot* are the kinds of affirmations we can make at any and every moment. The point is to accustom one's mind to the awareness of God as always in the background, whatever we may be doing in the moment. It is this combination of remembering and inner practice that allows us to do our spiritual work of renewal, exercising the care and responsibility it requires.

---

[22] See *Reb Ahrele's Heart*, translated and edited by Rabbis Hillel Goelman and Zalman Schachter-Shalomi, pp. 29-30.

Organicity / Endoskeletal

The other thing we have to think about in terms of the next generations is that *Yiddishkeit* must have the power to renew itself from the inside. If it is flexible enough then, as our children grow, they won't have to break out of a rigid container and be forced to discard so much of what could still be valuable. Rather, *Yiddishkeit* can expand and change with them, continuing its usefulness in providing meaning for their lives.

To accomplish this, we need to recognize that our *Yiddishkeit* has become too child-oriented. Paradoxically, because of being child-fixated, there are still so many people who have yet to experience a Passover *seder* for grownups. Seders for adults tend to be freer flowing and less inclined to focus only on the ritual and songs of the *haggadah* and therefore become vehicles for exploring contemporary meaning and renewal of old forms. This, in turn, gives children the same permission to explore both while they are still children and as they themselves become adults, contributing to the kind of *Yiddishkeit* about which I'm talking.[23]

What I am calling an "adult" *seder* is one which is open for intellectual and spiritual searching while still being something that children will recognize. Achieving this balance is not something that I can tell you how to do in the pages of a book, since each configuration of *seder* participants is unique. The children are of different ages, even the same children are a year older than they were the previous year, and each adult is in his or her unique moment in life. At the same time, I know that

---

[23] For example, Rabbi Arthur Waskow's "The Freedom Seder: A New Haggadah for Passover" was first used in 1969, one year after the assassination of the Reverend Martin Luther King, Jr. It juxtaposes traditional texts with relevant voices from that time. Since 1969, "The Freedom Seder" itself has been modified and dozens of other *haggadot* have been published which reflect the need to retain tradition while exploring relevance.

this is the genius of the *seder*, the genius of the way in which we manifest our *edut* / witnessing, these ways we have of celebrating who we are and who we are becoming. I know that the *seder*, as an example, contains within it multiple ways to achieve this balancing.

In this context, I also like to refer to the following discussion in the *Tanya* of Rabbi Schneur Zalman of Liadi.[24] He begins with the *passuk* / verse: "*Chanoch la-na'ar al pi darko, gam ki yazkin lo yassur mi-menu* / Educate the child according to his way, even when he will be old he will not depart from it."[25] Reb Schneur Zalman asks, "What kind of teaching is that? Do we want to teach children in such a way that when they get older, they will still follow the same paths they learned as children? Do we want to fix them at such an early moment in their development?

Reb Schneur Zalman responds to his own question by saying that this is not what the verse from Proverbs means. Rather, what we need to do is to teach children from the beginning in such a way that *Yiddishkeit* will have the ability to renew itself from the inside. Then, as they grow older, they won't have to break with the *Yiddishkeit* of their childhood and throw it away. Instead, their *Yiddishkeit* will grow as they grow and be able to stay with them.

In a sense, my complaint is not with the halachists of the past, who used the halachic method in ways which were appropriate for resolving the issues of their times. Rather, it is with the contemporary halachists who, by continuing to remain only within the older and established rules, have made *halachah*

---

[24] Rabbi Schneur Zalman of Liadi is the first rebbe of what is now known as Lubavitch or *Chabad Chassidut*. The *Tanya* includes the teachings and meditations forming the core of the *Chabad* approach which sees the Jew's central purpose as the unifying link between Creator and creation. This citation is from the introduction to the second unit of the *Tanya* called the *Sha'ar Ha-Yichud V-ha-Emunah* / Gate of Unity and Faith.

[25] Proverbs 22:6.

too rigid, too "bonelike" and more like an exoskeleton which is protective but cannot grow and change. Our task is to bring *halachah* back inside our collective body so that it can become more like an endoskeleton, surrounded by living flesh and skin. Deep within, we need absolutes, but around them we have to be able to grow, and that's what *chanoch la-na'ar* means.

LOVING ATTITUDE

It is not enough to incorporate updates into our practices. We also need to concern ourselves with the attitude we bring to these practices. This is because our attitude toward our behavior is the carrier wave that moves what is inside us into visibility. It is true that this word has recently come to have a different meaning. Having "attitude" has come to mean someone who is brash or abrasive. But, in a way, this change in how the word attitude is used does mean that people are becoming more aware that it's not only *what* one does but with what *attitude* one does it. This is what we learn from a study of the s'*firot*, and especially the seven *middot*, from the perspective of different aspects of personality. We need to bring an attention to attitude to our work and make sure that our communication is not only verbal but also expressive of love, focus, and compassion.[26] Again, attitude is the carrier wave for moving what is inside of us into visibility.

FEMINIST UNDERSTANDINGS

Another necessary and new contributor to the halachic process is a feminist approach to issues of practice. This includes both the analytic techniques being developed by women and an experiential way of understanding the essential core from which we can form opinions on contemporary questions. For example, I read a woman's description of a

---

[26] For example, a loving attitude expressed in specific behaviors would be a manifesting of the *middah* of *chesed*. Focus is *g'vurah* and compassion *tif'eret*.

dream she had. She was given a *torah* by *Malkitzedek* which she then took inside her body. But there was nothing written on the scroll. What I loved about this description is that she incorporated the white letters of the *torah* into herself. I think that deep experiences of this kind can be trusted to help us all make the shifts and do the reformatting that we have to do. The organicity and nurturing which come more from women's minds can help us stay on track and not go *m'shugah* / crazy as we all do this work. I deeply believe that feminist understanding has to become an important part of the halachic process.

DEVELOPMENTAL STAGES

What I am suggesting here both about the development of the halachic process through time and the changes we need to institute in order for this process to continue to mature, fits with the work of Lawrence Kohlberg and James Fowler. Each of them talked about six stages of moral and faith development in individuals which had to be experienced in sequence.[27] Thus, returning the text cited above, to say *"chanoch la-na'ar al pi darko,"* means that Torah and *mitzvot*, the way in which we do *halachah*, have to relate at all stages of a person's life. The same halachic practice needs to speak to the person in each stage of his/her moral development, providing a new perspective, a greater appreciation, and a deeper interpretation. This is why the concept of *pardes*, of interpreting Torah on multiple levels simultaneously, is so important for us.[28] It builds a ladder rather than a fixed point and helps us be consistent with Kohlberg's work of breaking down moral development into stages.

The same connection applies to Fowler's stages of faith development. He proposed that, when we are young, faith

---

[27] See http://en.wikipedia.org/wiki/Stages_of_faith_development and related articles as well as http://www.nd.edu/~rbarger/kohlberg.html.

[28] PaRDeS is an acronym for four words, *P'shat* / simple meaning, *Remez* / deductive, *Drash* / inductive and *Sod*/mystery.

works in a simple way. The person wants certain things and expects that, "The sugar daddy [i.e. God] will handle it all for me." Only much later in life can an individual arrive at a faith that is so deep that, "Yea, though He slay me, yet I will trust in Him."[29] To say that I trust in the transformative element that will finally take my life away and recycle it is such a different level than the first. Both these stages and all the stages in between are part of an organic way in which we come to understanding and we, as well as the greater halachic process, grow from one to the other.

The Four Cubits of Halachah

We have arrived at the place where we can begin to really understand how *halachah* has been done until now and, once having understood this better, to the beginning of an ability to use the principles of Integral Halachah in dealing with the issues we face.

In the Talmud, the source document for the classical rabbinic process, it says: *Mi-yom she-charav beit ha-mikdash ein lo l-ha-kadosh baruch hu b-olamo ela arba amot shel halachah bilvad /* Since the day the Holy Temple was destroyed, God has in His world only the four ells of *halachah*.[30]

What do they mean by saying that God's home in this world is limited to these *dalet /* four *amot* of *halachah*? Remember that the rabbis of the Talmud thought in terms of four levels of understanding anything in Torah. In *p'shat*, the literal meaning is pretty clear. The four cubits are my surround, one cubit in each of the four directions. I can count and say, "This is my space. I inhabit this space. It is my field." And so, the four cubit space of a person who lives life observing *halachah*

---

[29] Job 13:15.

[30] *B'rachot* 8a. *Amot*, or ells, is usually translated as cubits. Each cubit is about the length of an adult forearm. Four cubits would be about six to eight feet.

is the *beit ha-mikdash* seen as a field replacing structure. This is one meaning of what the *chachamim* meant when they articulated this idea. It's like a *kinyan* / an acquisition, where the person says that this area is part of my *guf* / body, it's my aura, my *makif ha-karov* / my immediate surround and all that is in it.

This leads to another question whose connection to the above will become clear as we proceed. I asked myself the following: "What happens if sometimes I *davven* at a different time than I put on *tallit* and *t'fillin*?[31] If that happens, then how long do I have to wear *tallit* and *t'fillin* in order to be *yotzei*?[32] Can I just put them on and then remove them immediately; or do I have to keep them on for a certain amount of time? The answer given in the sources is that I have to wear them, "*k'dei hiluch arba amot* / as long as it takes to walk four cubits."[33]

When I hear "as long as it takes to walk four cubits," I hear the four letters of the Divine Name and the four worlds they have come to represent in Kabbalistic and Chassidic teaching. In order to be *yotzei* on the *mitzvot* of *tallit* and *t'fillin*, I need to wear them at least as long as it takes me to ascend the four ells, to experience, however briefly, each of the four worlds. With the first step, the lower *hei*, I experience *assiyah*; with the second step, the *vav*, I experience *y'tzirah*; with the third step, the upper *hei*, I experience *b'ri'ah*, and with the fourth step, the *yod*, I experience *atzilut*. Then, I can remove the *tallit* and *t'fillin*.

---

[31] The *mitzvot* to say the morning *sh'ma* and *amidah* at set times can be separated from the *mitzvot* of putting on *tallit* and *t'fillin*. Therefore, it is possible to fulfill these *mitzvot* in different physical locations, as well as times.

[32] *Yotzei* is short for *la-tzeit y'dei chovato*, to exit from under the obligation. In other words, what is the minimum amount, here of time, needed to wear *tallit* and *t'fillin* in order to fulfill the *mitzvah*?

[33] This method of measuring time by distance is used in many places in rabbinic writing. In particular, see *Shulchan Aruch HaRav, Orach Chayim* 8:6 where Rabbi Schneur Zalman says that one needs to wrap oneself in a *tallit* for at least this time/distance and could, if s/he wanted, remove the *tallit* altogether after wearing it for this minimum time.

The rabbis also talk about *Shabbat* using a four fold system. Here, each letter of the Divine Name would correspond to one of four *r'shuyot* / domains that are discussed in relation to various prohibitions on *Shabbat* and which therefore connect with one another to create a complete reality. The *yod* is the *r'shut ha-yachid* / private domain; the *karmelit* / that which is between public and private domains corresponds to the upper *hei*; the *makom patur* / place which is exempt from restrictions altogether corresponds to the *vav*; and the *r'shut ha-rabbim* / public domain, is the lower *hei*.[34]

The first *mishnah* in Tractate *Shabbat* (2a) begins with the words, *y'tzi'ot ha-shabbat shtayim she-hen arba* / transfers [from one domain to another prohibited] on the Sabbath are of two types that expand to four. This applies to actions initiated either in the private or the public domain. This *mishnah* then gives an example of a poor person standing outside the door [in the public domain] and the *ba'al ha-bayit* / master of the house inside the door [in the private domain]. At the same time, we say that the *ani* / poor person is us and the *ba'al ha-bayit* is the *ribbono shel olam* / master of the world. As the poor person reaches inside to receive the gift, so we also reach into the Divine realms seeking the gift of the *Sh'chinah*'s presence in our lives. As the master of the house wants to give to the poor and so might reach his hand outside into the public domain, so God also can reach out to us, in the domain of *assiyah* in which we live. This is a chassidic understanding of the two primary *r'shuyot* in the context of our relationship with God.

So, what I plan to do in the rest of this book is to talk about these basic halachic texts and the principles that underly them. Then I want to ask, "Why was it suggested we do it this way? What did it mean to us at the time the suggestion was made?" I

---

[34] *Karmelit* is the most difficult domain to understand and seems to be in the air no more than ten handbreadths above the ground. *Makom patur* is the air higher than ten handbreadths.

believe that it is *k'dai* / worthwhile to put a lot of *ko'ach* / strength and *m'oach* / thought into this process because it will help us make the radical decisions about our own practice in an informed and loving way.

A Point to Seriously Consider

Before we move into these next areas, I have a very serious point I need to raise with you. After that, we can move into the first unit of the *Shulchan Aruch* called *Orach Chayyim* / the Way of Life.

Mashbi'a ani et talmidai li-hiyot ritzinim b-halachah / I adjure my students to be serious about *halachah*. *Ki achshav z'man ha-gibbush l-halachah l-idan ha-ba* / Now is the time we format the template of *halachah* for the future.

I understand Rupert Sheldrake to be offering a template from the world of biological and physical processes which can be applied to our work in *halachah*.[35] What he says is that when you create a new compound which then begins to crystallize, the form of the crystal is randomly determined. However, once nature gets entrained and makes it a habit to produce the crystal in a set form, then all the crystals that follow will take that shape.

This is the responsibility that we have now. *Ki achshav z'man ha-gibbush la-halachah l-idan ha-ba*, we are creating a pattern that will be reused for one *halachic* ruling after another. We are at the beginning of a new process which will be reused again and again.

---

[35] Rupert Sheldrake is a biologist who "has revolutionised scientific thinking with his vision of a living, developing universe with its own inherent memory." This quote is taken from his website, http://www.sheldrake.org/homepage.html where you can also find summaries of his work and the texts of many of his essays.

V-lo la-dun rak min ha-hergesh ha-atzma'i / [At the same time,] **Do not arrive at conclusions only from within feelings of independence** and freedom from the process as it has been until now, believing that you can make up your own mind on these questions without reference to and knowledge of what has come before. Functioning in this way is like being a grain of salt, drawing energy from its host but not nourishing it in return. I don't want Jewish Renewal to become a cancer on the body of the Jewish being. Rather, I want us to be a part of the living entity we call Judaism and living in harmony with that totality. I really want you to understand the importance of what I am saying. The people who are to the right and to the left of us are our organic brothers and sisters; we are co-cells with them in the Jewish body and the Jewish body is an organ that's co-organ with other organs in the body of humankind and that this organismic understanding has to be taken really seriously. We are not doing Jewish Renewal for ourselves alone. We are not doing it from an adolescent point-of-view. It may be true that in the sixties we were just in the here and now. Now, we need to become more conscious of the past and for our responsibility for the future. This is very important.

Talui ba-zeh harbeh / **So much depends on this;** *u-l'ma'an ha-shem lo yidonu eileh she ein la'hem kesher li-shmat'ta a'liba d-hilch'ta* / **for the sake of the Name, people who don't have a clear connection between what they have heard** and the halachic sources should not rule for others.[36] I take this to mean that those who haven't read *halachah* in the original, who haven't pursued it and followed it, should not rule for others.

Please be careful.

Please be careful.

---

[36] Reb Zalman is referencing a connection made in the Talmud between attaining a sense of serenity and knowing that that which one has heard is in conformity with *halachah* (*Sotah* 21a).

Don't rule for others; certainly not for others.

And for yourself, consult. Check it out.

Sometimes the greatest insights come from consulting the text in its original. This is because the text in the original gives us more breathing room than when we go to the definitions and the definitions of definitions that people who came to the text afterwards wrote.

I would also like to see discussions about practice done at a deeper level and more frequently, so that people start talking about "what should our consensus be about this issue and about that issue." I commend those of you who have been corresponding with each other on halachic matters as well as sharing your communities' processes through your *shul* newsletters, and especially for the conversations that take place on the various lists to which so many of you belong.

Va-ani m'ar-eyr al ha-talmidim she-da'atam kallah v-libam gas b-hora'ah / And I want to protest against those students whose mind concerning halachic things is careless and irresponsible. I did not stand up and defy so much convention in order to give people *s'michah* just to give permission to people to do things carelessly.

So please, please, be careful.

SHI'UR TWO: ORACH CHAYYIM

Baruch atah Yah lamdeini chukecha.
Ribono shel olam, ta'her libeinu l'ovd'cha be-met.
V-hanchileinu, Yah Eloheinu, torat chayyim v-a'havat chesed.

Praised are You, *Yah*: Teach me your statutes.
Master of all worlds, purify our hearts to serve You truthfully.
Give us as our heritage, *Yah* our God, a living Torah and love
of giving love.

Davvenen: Birchot Ha-Shachar

The first part of the four orders of the *Shulchan Aruch* is
called *Orach Chayyim* / Way of Life. In *Orach Chayyim*, there are
discussions about *hilchot hashkamat ha-boker* / laws for when one
gets up in the morning. This is one area where we have already
done a good deal of the work in Integral Halachah. For
example, as I was reading the material on *birchot ha-shachar* / the
morning blessings and about *davvennen* in general, I realized
that we have already done wonderful things in our *siddurim*.[1] As
we said in the introduction to *Or Chadash*,

> We must reintegrate body and soul so that they
> are organically in harmony...We enter the prayer
> via the way of the body at *Birchot Ha-Shachar* /
> dawn prayers...We get into our bodies, its

---

[1] The first *siddur* in Jewish Renewal was called *Or Chadash* / New Light. It
appeared in a loose-leaf format (which the current *Siddur Kol Koreh* also has)
and included instructions for movement as well as having cassettes of music.
It is no longer in print. There are now three primary Jewish Renewal
siddurim available, each with a different focus. See the ALEPH ReSources
Catalog for a list and descriptions.

passages and ducts, we attend to our breathing,
our posture and our stance.[2]

We introduced body movements to accompany the opening set
of morning *brachot* / blessings and this is a remarkable example
of what is possible when we apply the principles of Integral-
Halachah. In general, this is an area in which we have made
and continue to make good progress.[3]

T'fillin

When I look at the rulings and practices that have to do
with *t'fillin*, my sense is that this is a place where the consensus
may soon shift. We now find that there are good kids, about to
become *bar* or *bat mitzvah*, who don't want to have *t'fillin* made
from leather that cost an animal its life. Adults as well, who
want to take on the practice of wearing *t'fillin*, often share this
difficulty. But, according to tradition, you can't do it any other
way. It's *halachah l-moshe mi-sinai* / a practice which stretches all
the way back to Moses at Sinai to make *t'fillin* from leather.[4]

So my sense is that we need to be prepared for this *halachah
l-moshe mi-sinai*, this consensus, to shift. I do not think that this
shift will begin from the head, meaning from formally
constructed arguments made by knowledgeable leaders which

---

[2] "A New Approach: *Davvenology* and the Four Worlds," by Reb Zalman, *Or
Chadash*, Second Draft Edition, excerpted from pages intro 20 and intro 23 .

[3] At this point in the original video, Reb Zalman began to sing Rabbi Shefa
Gold's morning blessings whose refrain is "We're Rising in Remembrance
of Your Love." Movements for this were included on page 111 of Or
Chadash and the original recording is on "Songs of Renewal and
Jubilation."

[4] *Shabbat* 79b. There are several other references to aspects of *t'fillin* being
halachah l-moshe mi-sinai, such as the letters on the box for the head and the
four part division of that same box. For an expanded look at this issue, see
*Sacred Garment, Sacred Light: A Woman's Journey into the Jewish Ritual Garments of
Tefillin and Tallit*, by Rabbi Hanna Tiferet Siegel (June 1989), available from
the author (hannat@telus.net).

will then spread to the people. Rather, I think it will start from grass roots experiences and experiments as people look to deepen the meaning of their practice. For example, people who like to work with wood will find suitable precious hardwoods from which they will make their own *t'fillin* boxes. This is no less a renewable resource than animal skin and, by choosing the forests from where the wood comes, these *t'fillin* boxes can serve as a special connection to the ecology of that particular place. In so doing, the boxes themselves will reinforce the message of the second paragraph of the *sh'ma*, which so many of us now see as a call to ecological responsibility. And, while I can't at this moment see how to do this, it would be interesting to consider making ceramic *batim* / houses or boxes for *t'fillin*. What is easier to imagine is boxes and straps made from natural fiber cloths.

There are other possibilities which are closer to the classical approach and may be acceptable to many people. One is to use the skins of animals which died of natural causes rather than being slaughtered. I also realized that old *t'fillin* were made from rawhide, with which one can do many things not possible with tanned leather. We now have the technology to take leather from used *t'fillin*, chop it up finely, and take these leather particles and put it them together again using the same hydraulic press that produces the regular *batim* for *tefillin*. I would love to see all these possibilities explored.

For a period of time, I think the most important thing is to encourage people to experiment without needing to commit to any particular approach. For example, what would it be like for someone to write out the *parshiyot* / portions from the Torah that go into the *t'fillin* boxes by herself. Perhaps she would choose to write them on recycled paper rather than parchment or maybe even on paper that she made herself? Can you imagine the power of first contact with *t'fillin* if a *bar mitzvah bocher* / boy were required to learn how to make paper from fibers of cloth and then to inscribe the words of the *parshiyot* of the *t'fillin* on that paper, and finally sealing them inside the boxes himself? While these experiments would result in finished products that are departures from classical *halachah*, they would restore the traditional personal connection to this practice. If, in the end, this experimentation allows a new consensus of the pious to emerge which expands the range of acceptable *t'fillin*, then so much the better. If it doesn't, it will at least raise awareness of this powerful practice.

For all the above, what I am saying is that it's not an issue of waiting for someone else to give you permission to try something. Once people have actually experimented with other ways and have reported on their experiences, then the practice will begin to shift. I myself would like to put on such a pair of *t'fillin* to see what happens when I *davven* with them.

Between Solo and Minyan

Another thing that came up as I went through *Orach Chayyim* is the question of what constitutes a *minyan* / the quorum of a minimum of ten adult [males] which is required in order for certain prayers to be recited.[5] I would particularly like you to consider things that I pioneered for times when a *minyan* is not available and which I called "between solo and *minyan*." These include spending time in dyads, triads, and even groups of four and five.[6] Each one of these groups has a unique character and does different kinds of things.[7]

---

[5] For the most part, the prayers which require a *minyan* are those with a call and response that assumes the presence of a congregation, such as the *kaddish* and the *barchu*.

[6] Traditionally, if there is no *minyan*, then there is no group and each person prays as an individual. Reb Zalman is proposing that there are other options between these two end-points on the continuum of prayer.

[7] See the supplement at the end of this *shi'ur* for a fuller description of this form of *davvenen*.

At the same time as we work on these options for a kind of communal prayer without a minyan, we need to recognize that we have not yet fully learned how to constitute a *minyan* in its deeper meanings. On several occasions, I have asked people to stand in the formation of the *eitz ha-chayyim* / tree of life. In this way, each participant of the *minyan* became a different *s'firah* and this is how we *davvened* the *amidah*.[8] I remember this as being an amazing experience.

Another area of experimentation, then, is *davvenen* both with a *minyan* and with that which I call "between solo and *minyan*".

Siddur and Technology

I would like to see software designers create interactive programs for *davvenen*. Imagine a *siddur* that would give us the opportunity that, as we *davven* along, we could push the "enter" key each time we have said something and the program would continue by showing a deeper level of the same prayer we just experienced. The program would also have a "help" feature, so that you could get translations for words and explanations of concepts you didn't understand. Imagine, as well, what it would be like if we had the text of Psalm 148 on the screen.[9] As you said the opening words, "*Hall'lu et Adonai min ha-shamayim*" you would see a wonderful expanse of the sky and the Hebrew text would run from the center of the screen to the left and the English text from the center to the right.[10] When you got to the words, "*Eish u-varad sheleg v-kitor* / fire and hail, snow and fog,"

---

[8] See the *siddur, Ivdu et Hashem B'simcha* by Rabbi David Zaslow, pp. 243-246.

[9] This psalm begins with, "*Hall'luyah*! Praise God from the heavens" and which Reb Zalman often sings to "Michael Row the Boat Ashore" with *hall'luyah* as the repeating response to each phrase.

[10] This approach to the placement of text is used in *Siddur Kol Koreh*, whose early users reported that Reb Zalman's concept of Hebrew/English layout worked well for their eyes.

images of fire, hail, snow and fog would come up on screen, thereby helping the *davvener* to visualize the experience on which the Psalmist was drawing.

Shabbat: Servile Mechanisms

Next, I looked into *hilchot Shabbat* / the laws of the Sabbath, and how to relate to what I would call servile mechanisms.

Let me start with an example that seems somewhat ironic, namely, the use of a dishwasher on *Shabbat*.

Here is what makes this issue ironic. As it stands, classical *halachah* creates a funny situation: During the week, you have fewer guests and so you have fewer dishes to wash. Not only are there fewer dishes, but washing them by hand is easier than using the dishwasher. On *Shabbat*, when you have *orchim* / guests in the house, should you at that point say, "No, I'm not going to use the dishwasher when I need it the most? And *davka* / precisely at that point when it would allow me to have more *Shabbat* rather than less." Therefore, my first thought is that it should be okay to use a dishwasher on *Shabbat*.

On the other hand, believing that this is the right thing to do raises the question of how to implement this change. In halachic language, using a dishwasher on *Shabbat* should require a *shinui* / change in the usual way one uses such a mechanism, a *shabbosdik* way.[11] If I use the dishwasher on *Shabbat* in the same way as I do during the week, then it's not right.

On the other hand, I know that a strong case is made for the idea that *Shabbat* is a day to allow the world to be as it is with minimum human interference. Operating within that assumption, it follows that we should not use electricity and the servile mechanisms that are dependent on it.

---

[11] For example, if one holds a pen in his/her fingers, but then turns the hand backwards, this is considered a *shinui* and, while not exactly permitting one to write on *Shabbat*, it at least is not forbidden. See *Shabbat* 104b.

There is a *klal* / general principle that says, *"Psik reisha v-lo yamut* / If you cut off the head, will it not die?"[12] If we apply this principle to the use of servile mechanisms, then the conclusion is that they cannot be used. For example, if I open the refrigerator door, the light goes on. Since opening the door creates the necessity for the light to turn on, then there is no doubt that I caused it and so I cannot say, "I didn't mean for the light to go on; I only wanted to get inside." The action of opening the door causes the light to turn on. That's why this is an example of *psik reisha* – if you cut off its head, *v-lo yamut* – won't it die? So this is very strong argument for not disconnecting causal actions one from another.

Maybe it would be better if we just not activate these things on *Shabbat.* I don't have an answer yet, but I would like to see people experiment with answering this question and to start reporting the ways they find that work for them.

Shabbat: Defining M'lachah

If we continue to follow this line of reasoning, then maybe we have to start thinking differently about servile mechanisms.[13] In turn, this means going all the way back to the starting place of this reasoning, which is what we define as a *m'lachah* / work that is prohibited on Shabbat.[14]

One idea I had about a possible redefinition of *m'lachah* came to me when I thought about the furor around some of President Clinton's cabinet appointees. It came out that they

---

[12] See, for example, *Shabbat* 75a.

[13] In arguing backwards from a conclusion already reached through ethical reasoning, Reb Zalman is firmly within the halachic tradition. For other examples of how this works, see *Not in Heaven* by Eliezer Berkovits.

[14] The Torah tells us only not to do any work or have a fire on Shabbat. The rabbis take these references and, because they appear close to descriptions of the work done to build the desert tabernacle, define *m'lachah* as anything that was done to build or maintain the Temple ritual. (*Chagigah* 10b).

had hired domestic workers but had not paid into social security for them. What occurred to me was that maybe we could define *m'lachah* today as that kind of work which requires the employer to pay into social security and therefore is forbidden on Shabbat. If it turned out that this idea was accepted, it would lead to a whole new reformulation of what is *m'lachah* which would have implications for which things one could do oneself and which things one must delegate. That which you delegate is what the Torah calls *m'lechet avodah* / "of a slave"-work.[15] So, I would like us to come up with a new understanding of *m'lachah* which would lead to the formulation of a *shabbosdike* way of using servile mechanisms that avoids doing a *m'lachah*. This is one way to apply the process of Integral Halachah to *hilchot Shabbat*, that is, to start at first principles and then redefine the specifics in their light.

Another way to renew *hilchot Shabbat* is to ask pragmatically: "What is the practice?" Some people will have the practice of not using electricity on *Shabbat* and therefore not using servile mechanisms either. It will be very helpful to this larger process when they report back on how this works for them and in what ways it enhances their *Shabbat* experience. There will be others who will find a *shabbosdike* way of using servile mechanisms and it will be equally helpful to the larger process when they report back. Having more information about different forms of practice will help us all to get this together.

Music on Shabbat

It is a given of classical *halachah* that it is forbidden to play musical instruments on *Shabbat*. There is a difference of opinion about why. One point of view is that the prohibition is

---

[15] The prohibition on Shabbat is *kol m'lachah* / all work. On a holiday it is *kol m'lechet avodah*. For example, a person may neither start a fire on *Shabbat* nor transfer it. On a holiday, however, while a person still can't start a fire, s/he can raise or lower it or transfer it from one wick to another.

essentially *mi-d'oraita* / from the Torah and has to do with avoiding the possibility of fixing or tuning an instrument on *Shabbat*.[16] The other point of view is that it is essentially *mi-d'rabbanan* / rabbinic and has more to do with a practice that is a response to the destruction of the temple.[17]

Some modern people are adamant that the prohibition is *mi-d'oraita* because they so opposed organs in Reform temples that they marshaled every argument they could to stop this practice. From my point of view, they were throwing the kitchen sink at the reformers over something which really isn't that fundamental. It was like saying that using an organ on *Shabbat* was itself *avodah zarah* / idol worship, because it leads to *gilui arayot* / sexual immorality and even *sh'fichat damim* / the spilling of blood. Don't do this because the Torah itself is against the practice.

On the other side, the Psalm for the *Shabbat* Day itself says, *"Tov l-hodot la-shem...alay asor v-alay navel* / It is good to thank God...on the ten-string lyre and the harp" and all the other instruments mentioned there.[18]

Again, my conclusion is that, where we are today, and how little time we have for celebrating in a musical way, musical instruments are a very *shabbosdike* thing. Based on our redefinition of *m'lachah*, however that comes out, we will need to also redefine why it is and in what ways it is permissible to use musical instruments on *Shabbat*. One thing I already know is that just before we begin using an instrument we should say, *Baruch she-amar* and when we are finished we say *yishtabach*.[19]

---

[16] *Beitzah* 36b and *Bet Yosef, Orach Chayyim* 339:3.

[17] *Shulchan Aruch Orach Chayyim* 560:3. Also, *Eruvin* 104a and *Shulchan Aruch Orach Chayyim* 338:5.

[18] Psalm 92.

[19] These are the opening and closing paragraphs of *Psukei D'zimra* / Verses

Let me share with you an experience I had. I once was a *Shabbat* guest in the home of a liberal orthodox rabbi. Before *Shabbat* began, I took the arm of the record player and lifted it off to the side and started the turntable. I put a recording of the "Chichester Psalms" by Bernstein on the moving turntable and turned on the amplifier and set the sound levels. After dinner, I invited the people to come and sit around and I put the needle above the first groove. Just before the music began, I said these words from *Baruch She'amar*:

> *Got, ha-el ha-av ha-rachaman ha-m'hullal b'fi amo, m'shubach u-m'fo'ar b-l'shon chasidov va-avadav, u-v-shirey david avdecha, nihalelcha u-n'shabechacha, u-n'fa'ercha v-nazkir shimcha... yachid chei ha-olamim, melech m'shubach... melech m'hulal ba-tishbachot* / God, the Highest, Merciful parent who is extolled by the people, praised and glorified by the tongue of the pious ones and servants. And through the songs of David, Your servant, we will extol You Holy One, our God, with praises and psalms. We will exalt, praise and glorify You. We will talk about the four letter Name and proclaim You our guide, our God, Unique One, Life of the Realms, Ruler, praised and glorified forever is the Great Name...Who is extolled [in return] with [the speech of] our praises.[20]

Then I put the needle on and we listened to the three psalms – which are so beautiful. When it was over, I picked up the needle and I said, *"Yishtabach shimcha la'ad malkeinu* / **Your name be**

---

of Praise, the section of the morning service that precedes the *Sh'ma* and its blessings. *Baruch She-amar* talks about praising God in the words of the psalmist and *yishtabach* mentions how praising God in different forms is exactly what God most wants from us. (ds)

[20] Translation by Rabbi Zalman Schachter-Shalomi.

praised without end, majestic One." Thus, I framed listening to sacred music on *Shabbat* within the parameters of *p'sukei d'zimra* and made it clear that listening to this music on *Shabbat* was truly in praise of God.

I do think that a family listening to music together is an important kind of bonding which is appropriate for *Shabbat*. So, again, I would like us to discuss where the limits should be. Where would rap or rock music fit? Which kinds of music are *shabbosdik* and which ones are not? Some people will say, "Only if the music to which you are listening is done by living people who are physically present, live music, can you listen to it on *Shabbat*. But if it is recorded music, then it is forbidden." But then, what happens to people who appreciate music but who don't themselves play instruments? Should they not be able to listen to the recorded music they love *l-koved Shabbos?*

Recording the Sacred

For those of us who make recordings of sacred music and Torah, there are things that can be done to deepen the experience of both producing and listening. For example, given that multiple tracks can be put on a recording one by one, I will put one voice on one track and another voice on the other track; sometimes I do Hebrew on one track, and English on the other.[21] I do this because what is really important is to put your inner experience into the recording and using the available technology can help.

I'm not sure that I really know how to do this. I do know that all the recordings that I have made for people, whether it's davvenology, singing, or *chassidic* teachings and stories, I created with deep *kavvanah* so that people who listen to them will be

---

[21] One example of this is Reb Zalman's audio *siddur, Davvening with Reb Zalman*, available from the ALEPH ReSources Catalog.

able to access that *kavvanah*. My goal was to incorporate embedded vibes as best I could.

If I knew how, I might even try to do this in a subliminal way, putting in those little, tiny blips that can hardly be heard. Each "blip" would be a variation on the intention to pray or learn for a higher purpose. One would be, "*li-shem yichud kudsha brich hu* / for the sake of unifying the Holy One (with the *Sh'chinah*);" another, "for the healing of the planet." There could be a series of these deep *kavvanot* so that the person who is listening would hear them and be able to intend that same *kavvanah*. In that way, the *sod* / hidden part of whatever the recording was, that which is embedded in the text or story or prayer, would become manifest.

This, also, requires discussion, because we need to think through the issues raised in other circles about the recording of prayer and Torah. Is it acceptable to use the Divine Name in a recording? Can we record services live, even on *Shabbat*? To what extent can a recording be used for an actual experience of prayer when a person cannot find a community with which to pray?[22]

Yom Tov Sheni

The issue of whether to retain, renew, or let go of *yom tov sheni shel galuyot* / the second day of a holiday in the exile[23] is

---

[22] Since Reb Zalman first made these suggestions, recordings of services in a Jewish Renewal context have been made. See the ALEPH ReSources Catalog for some of these.

[23] Because the new month was declared only after the new moon had been sighted by two witnesses, notification often arrived late in communities far from Jerusalem. Therefore, these communities would observe the major holidays for two days instead of one, knowing that one of those two days was in fact the holiday. The mathematical formula for determining the calendar was released by Hillel the Second in the 4th century. Since then, all communities know exactly when the holiday is, but diaspora communities retained the "extra" day as a sign of exile.

one that I think needs to be engaged in a conscious way. At this point, we are dealing with it mostly by simple omission. There was a time in my life when it looked like my family and I were going to make *aliyah*. We had gone to Israel for visits and had lived there for half a year and began to set things up for our permanent move. I was on the level of *da'ato lachzor la-aretz /* one whose mind is set to return to the land and therefore I was observing only one day of *yom tov*, which is the practice both for Jews actually living in Israel as well as Jews who view their presence outside of Israel as temporary. There is something that says to me that this criterion for relating to the second day of a *yom tov* isn't enough, nor is it satisfactory to continue observing the second day as it's been celebrated in the past.

I think that what I've studied in *chassidus* provides a clue to a new way of thinking about this second day. Chassidim stress the importance of the second day of *yom tov* in *chutz la-aretz /* the diaspora because of the differences in the way the Divine *shefa* flows outside of Israel and the doubt-producing controversy it generates. It seems especially interesting to celebrate a holiday whose source is doubt.[24]

I was once celebrating how important *safek /* doubt is and I said that, if we didn't have doubt, our faith would grow barnacles. So Rabbi Meyer Fund said, "Well, if doubt is such a great thing, then we should have a *yom tov* for doubt!" Then he added, "We do have such a holiday! We have the second day of *yom tov* because it's *s'feka d-yoma /* a day which is in doubt!" So, I think we might call this extra day of *yom tov, yoma d-sfeka*, the celebration of the "Ain't necessarily so." It can be a day on which we can do a little bit of debunking which would be very healthy for us.

---

[24] See *Likkutei Halachot, Hilchot T'fillat HaMinchah* 6:12.

Yom Tov Sheni: Sustainable Ecology

Another approach to the second day of *yom tov* would be ecological. Let's take the holiday of *Shavu'ot* as an example. On the first day, we would go to *shul* like we do now. We would hear the ten commandments read and even say *yizkor*.[25] At the same time, part of *Shavu'ot* has to do with the outdoors, with green, with its being *chag ha-katzir* / the holiday of cutting and harvesting wheat.[26] So, the second day of *Shavu'ot* could be celebrated outdoors, beginning with *davvenen* followed by a picnic.

Each of the major *yom tovim* / holidays has an important ecological component and teaching that celebrating the second, or extra days of each of them with ecology as its focus is something worth considering seriously. This would tie each holiday to its natural season and encourage us to develop observances that focus on *chagei ha-shanah k-efsharut l-chaven tikkunim l-ripui ha-teva* / the holidays of the year as a chance to intend correctives for the healing of nature. And I want to emphasize that these practices should be done with the *kahal* / community. I'm not saying that it should be just a picnic. In a way, the existing model would be *Tu B-sh'vat* and the way we plant trees and have an ecologically focused *seder* on that day.

Yom Tov Sheni: Awareness of Earth Connections

Another, related possibility comes from the way a Hopi man once responded to my descriptions of *Pesach* and *Sukkot*. After I explained to him what these holidays are about, he said,

> I get it. You people don't want to be slaves, so you say to your kids, "We can't stay in this place. We've got to go away." And the kids ask, "What

---

[25] Which is usually said on the second day.

[26] There is a custom to decorate the synagogue with branches on *Shavu'ot*.

are we going to eat?" So you say, "I'm going to
show you." You take a sheep and you roast it. You
find some dandelion greens and you crack some
wheat and bake it on a stone. "That's what we're
going to eat on our way as we leave this place."

Then they ask, "Where are we going to sleep?
Where are we going to stay?" So you have that
holiday in the fall – *Sukkot* – where you show them
that you build a lean-to and you will stay inside.
So you've shown the children how you will take
care of shelter and food.

I thought this was a wonderful insight into a dimension of these
holidays and that we could use the second days of *yom tov* to
increase our awareness of earth connections.

Yom Tov Sheni: Permeable Membranes / Hyphenation

Another way to give meaning to the second day of *yom tov*
would be as a day in which we acknowledge our permeability
to other spiritual practices. All of us are at least a little
hyphenated. Some of us are drawn to Sufism and others to
Buddhism; some to yoga and some to tai chi; some to
Hinduism and some to Native American practices. In one way
or another, we all have a little bit of something other than
Jewish that is a meaningful part of us. So, *yom tov sheni* could
celebrate that hyphenation by using that part of the other paths
to which we are drawn to observe our Jewish holiday.

For example, I realize that *Yom Kippur* can only be one day.
But if *Yom Kippur* could have a second day, it could be for
kundalini yoga, for going out through the chakra on the top,
keter. More realistically, a family that likes Native American
things could celebrate the second day of *Shavu'ot* in a way that
draws upon a practice I know some have of a summer solstice
prayer day to help the sun across the sky. And, since we are

already going to a body of water for *tashlich*, what if we did so on the second day of *Rosh Hashanah* and *davvened* the entire liturgy outdoors on the banks of a river? These are the some of the possibilities which come to mind when I think about yom *tov sheni shel galuyot*.

Transplanting non-Jewish into Jewish

This discussion of *yom tov sheni* and its possibilities leads us into the important question of, "What can we incorporate from other paths and what can we not incorporate?" In the first *shi'ur* I said that Judaism needs anchors – absolutes, non-negotiables, and basic boundaries. Without these boundaries, Judaism falls apart. I said that we have to watch the immune system and to take great care with what we change and what we import.

Now I'm talking in a way that could lead to many transplants. If you were to ask me what I think will happen to our immune system if we incorporate all these things, my answer would be that I don't know for sure.

This does lead me back to something I said in the first *shi'ur* and that is to go slowly and carefully. At the same time, I do want us to share what we have with others and to receive from others as well, so that we become like a laboratory for an experiment in both establishing and crossing boundaries.

I was looking in the *Rambam* and saw how concerned he is about the issues of staying away from *avodah zarah* / lit. foreign worship or idolatry and how connected and aware one needs to be about *yichud Hashem* / the unity of God. He spends a lot of time detailing the *mitzvot* that deal with the boundary of what's Jewish and what is idolatry.[27] I take his concern about boundaries seriously. I have been trying, and continue to try, to experience this deep in my *kishkes*, deep inside myself, to pray it through, to meditate it through, and here's what comes to me:

----

[27] In *Sefer Ha-Mada, Hilchot Y'sodei ha-Torah* and *Hilchot Avodat Kochavim.*

There is something about Zen that is Japanese and there is something about Zen that is universal. There is something about Hinduism that is Indian and there is something about Hinduism that is universal. That which is universal, that which is not particularly ethnic, is not *zarah*, is not *avodah zarah*. That which *is* particularly ethnic, that which belongs to a whole other genetic structure as it were, to a whole other morphogenic field, that is *zarah* and to practice it would be *avodah zarah*. Those are the things we should leave alone.

There is so much that I want to learn from Native Americans, particularly ways to honor our mother the earth. But I don't aspire to a *shtreimel* made of feathers in which to *davven*. I do want to use a drum at *davvenen*, but not necessarily the same drum that is used in the teepee for a peyote meeting.

My sense it that we honor that part of others' practice which is wholly ethnic when we enter that practice as guests; when we treat it like guests do. We should thank our friends for the glimpse they have given us of God through their window, recognizing that it is not our window. We have to filter out the universal from the ethnic, importing the universal while leaving the ethnic to those to whom it rightfully belongs. It is something like saying, "I can take the plasma of blood, but I can't take whole blood transfusions."

Transplanting Jewish into non-Jewish

This leads me to the opposite question, "What can we give to other people?"

There are certain Jewish structures that are universal and their importance lies in the way in which they are educational. They are good frames on which you can build, like sculptors who put a wire skeleton on the inside of what will become the sculpture and then they build around that.

The *seder* is this kind of a spiritual scaffolding. I have helped Christians to develop a Christmas *seder*, which included the same four cups and the same structure of the four parts to the *seder*. The first cup is the *yod* of the Divine name and represents the sanctification of the Christmas time and space. The second cup is the *hei*, which is telling the story. In a Christmas *seder*, the story is the story of the nativity, so here is where the particularity of the "sculpture" is expressed over the universal skeleton. When I talked with Buddhists, the particular story is the life of the Buddha, how he was born and how he gained his enlightenment. In each case, there were things on the table that we pointed to and said that we will be eating it, and why.

Sharing the concept of a *seder* with Christians made such a wonderful impact. It showed a caring for the spiritual path of another and provided a way of renewing Christmas for those for whom the celebration of Christmas has become the turkey and the opening of presents; where it has been all but forgotten whose birth they are celebrating and what that birth means. Buddhists also appreciated this structure as a marvelous way to tell their story, because it turns it into a household rather than a temple ceremony.

Conclusion

These are some of the things that I think about in relation to *Shulchan Aruch Orach Chayyim*. I share them not as definitive, not as another legal code, but as catalysts for conversation about these and the many other topics of concern that are part of this unit of the *Shulchan Aruch*.

Orach Chayyim
Appendix A: "From Solo to Minyan"

In suggesting places where dyadic and other small-group ways of *davvenen* might be especially useful, we are affirming the belief that we are parts of God and that we can sometimes more easily contact the divine within the other-with-whom we *davven* than the divine within ourselves. While some of us are adept enough to bypass the ego's blockade of the access to the Divine Self directly, most of us find it easier to do this by addressing the divine in each other. The signs will be graphic and clear. While one can *davven* the sections so marked by oneself in solo or choral fashion, we have found that it works so much better when done as dyadic I-Thou dialogues.

When we work in dyads, we do responses focusing on the God within the other, and recite alternating between partners. Dyads are also used in other phases of the *davvenen*. For instance: during the *Sh'ma* and its blessings, one partner reads while the other is free to concentrate on the non-verbal and visual elements of prayer. Then they can either switch or make affirmations. One person begins by stating half a sentence and the other finishes it. This often opens both to surprise and astonishment. Or, use the following form:

Person 1: *Sh'ma* + (name of partner)

Together: *Y*AH *Eloheynu*

Person 2: *Sh'ma* + (name of partner)

Together: *Y*AH *Eloheynu*

Person 1: *Y*AH *Echad/Achat*!

Repeated challenge and naming raises the partner to heightened awareness.

In triads, as in dyads, the partners alternate. For example:

Person 1: *YAH melech*

Person 2: *YAH malach*

Person 3: *YAH yimloch*

Together: *l-olam va'ed*!

At times when more appropriate, e.g., working with a group of Jews and non-Jews, we might use a chant like:

Person 1: "The fullness of God

Person 2: the void is God.

Person 3: This moment God

Together: and eternity."

    or

Person 1: "It is perfect

Person 2: You are loved

Person 3: All is clear

Together: and I am holy."

At times we form a Magen David of two triads; a powerful exercise.

We welcome you to explore, expand the parameters of your own ways of *davvenen* and to joyfully approach the human-God and human-human encounter with all your body, "all your heart, all your mind and all your soul."

(*Or Chadash*, pp. 27-28)

Orach Chayyim
Appendix B: Eating *Kitniyot* (Legumes) on *Pesach* (OH 453:1)

Question:

In light of the ingathering of the exiles, would it be possible to eliminate the Ashkenazic custom of not eating legumes on Pesach?

Responsum:

1) In our opinion it is permitted (and perhaps even obligatory) to eliminate this custom. It is in direct contradiction to an explicit decision in the Babylonian Talmud (*Pesahim* 114b) and is also in contradiction to the opinion of all the sages of the Mishnah and Talmud except one (R.Yochanan ben Nuri, *Pesahim* 35a and parallels). It also contradicts the theory and the practice of the *Amoraim* both in Babylonia and in Israel (*Pesahim* 114b and other sources), the *Geonim* (*Sheiltot, Halakhot Pesukot, Halakhot Gedolot*, etc.) and of most of the early medieval authorities in all countries (altogether more than 50 *Rishonim*!).

2) This custom is mentioned for the first time in France and Provence in the beginning of the thirteenth century by R. Asher of Lunel, R. Samuel of Falaise, and R. Peretz of Corbeil – from there it spread to various countries and the list of prohibited foods continued to expand. Nevertheless, the reason for the custom was unknown and as a result many sages invented at least eleven different explanations for the custom. As a result, R. Samuel of Falaise, one of the first to mention it, referred to it as a "mistaken custom" and R. Yerucham called it a "foolish custom".

3) Therefore, the main halakhic question in this case is whether it is permissible to do away with a mistaken or foolish custom. Many rabbinic authorities have ruled that it is permitted (and perhaps even obligatory) to do away with this type of "foolish custom" (R. Abin in *Yerushalmi Pesahim*, Maimonides, the Rosh, the Ribash, and many others). Furthermore, there are many good reasons to do away with this "foolish custom": a) It detracts from the joy of the holiday by limiting the number of permitted foods; b) It causes exorbitant price rises, which result in "major financial loss" and, as is well known, "the Torah takes pity on the people of Israel's money"; c) It emphasizes the insignificant (legumes) and ignores the significant (*hametz*, which is forbidden from the five kinds of grain); d) It causes people to scoff at the commandments in general and at the prohibition of *hametz* in particular – if this custom has no purpose and is observed, then there is no reason to observe other commandments; e) Finally, it causes unnecessary divisions between Israel's different ethnic groups. On the other hand, there is only one reason to observe this custom: the desire to preserve an old custom. Obviously, this desire does not override all that was mentioned above. Therefore, both Ashkenazim and Sephardim are permitted to eat legumes and rice on *Pesah* without fear of transgressing any prohibition.

4) Undoubtedly, there will be Ashkenazim who will want to stick to the "custom of their ancestors" even though they know that it is permitted to eat legumes on *Pesah*. To them we recommend that they observe only the original custom of not eating rice and legumes but that they use oil from legumes and all the other foods "forbidden" over the years, such as peas, beans, garlic, mustard, sunflower seeds, peanuts etc. Thus they will be able to eat hundreds of products, which bear the label "Kosher for *Pesah* for those who eat legumes." This will make

their lives easier and will add joy and pleasure to their observance of *Pesah*.

Rabbi David Golinkin

Approved Unanimously 5749

Reprinted with the permission of the Rabbinical Assembly of Israel, Masorti Movement. The full, Hebrew text of this responsum is available at http://www.responsafortoday.com/vol3/4.pdf

SHI'UR THREE: YOREH DE'AH

V-taher libenu l-ovdecha be-emet. L'ma'an lo niga la-rik v-lo neled la-behalah. Mi zeh ha-ish y're ha-shem. yoreinu b-derech yivchar.

Purify our hearts to serve You in truth (From the liturgy)
That we not labor in vain nor bring forth in dismay (Isaiah 65:23)
Whoever fears God will be shown what path to choose.

(Psalm 25:12)

Note On Methodology

As you read, I encourage you to write down the concerns that arise in relation to the suggestions I'm making. Discuss them with a close friend and learning partner. Ask yourselves how to deal with these concerns, identify the sources with which to research them, and how you would apply these sources. Finally, think about how you would design spiritual experiments and experiences to discover what actually works for you.

I write this because I remember a conversation I had with a close friend who was involved in the early retreats of *P'nai Or.*[1] During that period of time, we used to have these wonderful planning meetings where we opened up everything for examination and restructured the liturgical processes for our use. I asked him if he remembered the process by which we designed our *Rosh HaShanah* experience, the discussion which led us into talking about the deep structure of *Rosh HaShanah*, how one enters fully into that structure, and what one would need to do today to experience the original intent which created the liturgy that we inherited.

---

[1] *P'nai Or*, which succeeded *B'nai Or*, was the precursor of ALEPH.

This process of opening up the liturgy for examination and restructuring was amazing and we did this for other holidays as well. My friend and his wife were among the pioneers of what we did at Fellowship House Farm near Philadelphia, where we designed the *Simchat Torah* retreat, for example, and the various dances we choreographed for each of the *hakkafot*.[2]

So I asked him if he could recall our conversations and spend some time writing down his memories of the things we had discussed and the methods we had used. Unfortunately, these details were lost to him and to me and it is too bad that we didn't record them as they were happening. This is why I encourage you to record your concerns and thoughts as you read and share them with friends, so that the process is remembered as well as the results.

In addition, I think what I'm trying to say about Integral Halachah is that the methodology is at least as important as the conclusions. If we record how we approach the needed updates, then how we actually accomplish the transformation, translating old into new in a way that makes sense and allows us to go forward with integrity, then we will have captured the process and made it explicit.

Yoreh De'ah

Now it is time to take a look at *Shulchan Aruch Yoreh De'ah*, the second "movement," if you will, in the four movements which make up the *Shulchan Aruch*. This unit, whose title means "Teaching Knowledge (or, Let Him Show us Understanding)," deals with issues relating to kosher food, to the separation of *milchig* / dairy and *fleishig* / meat. It also details the procedures for *gerut* / conversion or initiation into Judaism and describes

---

[2] *Hakkafot*, literally the circling. On *Simchat Torah*, the holiday when the reading of the Torah is both completed and begun again, it is customary to remove all the Torah scrolls from the ark and walk with them around the synagogue seven times.

how to build a *mikveh* / ritual bath as well as many other areas of Jewish practice.

These are the thoughts that come to me relating to the subjects of this section:

Sh'chitah / Slaughtering

I used to be a *shochet* / slaughterer, going into the slaughter house to *shecht* / slaughter chickens. What I saw was that the suppliers didn't see these chickens as living beings, only as merchandise. They were dropped off, alive, in cages. They had not been fed any water, were dust dry, and screaming. So the first thing I did was to put some water in their cages.

Then I would send everybody out and start talking to the chickens: "You know, I'm not just here to kill you. I'm here to help you move to the next level in the journey between *chai* and *m'dabber*."[3] What I was trying to do was give them an invitation to continue moving from the animal toward the human.

The next thing I did was to offer both a *kavvanah* / intention and a *brachah* / blessing: "*Halevai* / let it be that somebody should eat you *l-koved Shabbos* / to honor Shabbat and use the energy s/he gets from you to *davven* a strong *nishmat kol chai* / the breath of all that lives so that your life, your body, your substance becomes elevated and the sparks in you become raised." I took what I had learned in *chassidus* really seriously, tried to apply it in real situations, and I continue in this tradition.

---

[3] The world divides into four levels of existence which are: *domem* / silent (i.e., inorganic), *tzome'ach* / growing (i.e., vegetation), *chai* / alive (i.e., animal), and *m'dabber* / speaking (i.e., human). Each level is higher than the previous one moving from *domem*, the lowest, to *m'dabber*, the highest. (One source for this division is *Sefer Miftachey Chochmat Ha-emet*, Saul Baumann, chapter 29, p. 53.) (srf)

Only then would I check the *chalef* / knife to make sure it was both *chad* / sharp and *chalak* / smooth and without nicks. Next I took the first bird and did the *t'fisah* / proper holding of the neck so that the *simmanim* / signs of a kosher slaughter, the gullet and the windpipe, would be prominent. When these are cut, it is almost inevitable that the *shochet* also cuts the arteries and veins which feed oxygen to the brain. Finally, I made the first *brachah* and did the *sh'chitah* itself.[4]

When I had finished this preparation and killed the first chicken, I would invite the people who were the pluckers to return. I didn't wanted their consciousness to impede on mine when I was tuning in to the *sh'chitah* itself. They used to call me the "Bee-bop Rabbi" because I would sing spirituals with the chicken pluckers so that we could all get into a better frame of mind than the one we would have had if we engaged in banter or listened to the radio as we worked.

Kosher and Eco-Kosher

Since those days, I have spent a lot of time thinking about this issue of keeping *kosher* and of *sh'chitah* in particular. For many years now, people have asked me, "How do you deal with the issue of *sh'chitah* today?" Most of us who buy *kosher* meats in the market get them already kashered and frozen. Not so long ago, we bought our kosher meat from a butcher and took it home to soak and salt it ourselves and, in so doing, complete the kashering process that began with the *sh'chitah*. It is easy for us, just as it was for those suppliers of the live chickens, to see the meat simply as another form of produce because we are removed from the flow which begins with a living animal.

---

[4] There are two *brachot* which must be said during the slaughtering process. The first is for the slaughter and the second is for covering the blood. These are the primary tools for elevating the action to the spiritual. (ds)

This disconnection creates space for practices which, while perhaps economically viable, raise questions about whether the *halachot* of *kashrut* go far enough to keep us in contact with the meaning of *kashrut*. For example, I remember when the first articles were published in Jewish periodicals about the methods by which calves were raised for veal. They were tightly penned-in, lived in perpetual darkness, force fed milk long after they should have been weaned and given animal fat. They were seen as just bio-machines that grow meat. This was really a sad situation and led to a revolt by Jewish consumers who refused to buy veal until the practices were changed to become more humane. This represented one of the early ways in which eco-*kashrut* began – by invoking the principle of *tza'ar ba'alei chayyim* / the **suffering of living beings** as an integral part of what it means to say that meat is *kosher*.[5]

The other modern issue over *sh'chitah* is that every so often a government will forbid *sh'chitah* altogether. Sometimes that is for anti-Semitic reasons, like the prohibition against *sh'chitah* in Nazi Germany. In most other cases, however, it is because the government requires stunning the animals before slaughtering. This is the situation in some European countries now, such as Sweden, Norway, Iceland, and Switzerland.[6]

---

[5] The principle of avoiding giving an animal unnecessary pain is invoked in several places in the Babylonian Talmud. One of the principle source texts is the Torah's injunction to help your enemy relieve the load on an animal that has fallen because the load it carries is too heavy (*Bava M'tzi'a* 31a).

In the case of veal, there are rabbinic authorities who, while recognizing the violation of *tza'ar ba'alei chayyim*, still separate that from the question of whether the animal is kosher (Chabad {http://www.chabad.org/library/article.asp?AID=60319#comments} and the Orthodox Union {http://oukosher.org/index.php/faqs/single/veal/}). Others, including the great modern *posek* / decisor Rav Moshe Feinstein z"l, forbid eating veal (see http://www.kosherblog.net/2006/11/02/faq-is-kosher-meat-better/ for this reference and for other material dealing with consumer reactions).

[6] Http://en.wikipedia.org/wiki/Bans_on_ritual_slaughter

This is an issue because, *al pi din* / according to law, stunning knocks the animal out and there is a big difference between an animal that is unconscious and one that is conscious. In the case of an animal which is unconscious, there is a *chashash* / fear that it might be *treifah* / not kosher because it may have sustained a fatal injury during the stunning and thus would no longer qualify as being *bar kayama* / viable to [continue to] exist. Therefore, we have considered stunning to be wrong since we can only slaughter an animal which we know is still capable of living on its own.

Also, I've seen some of the ways in which people have stunned animals, such as simply hitting the animal over the head with a sledge hammer, which isn't an improvement. Today, most places stun by means of an electric shock which knocks them out before they're actually butchered. (Notice the difference between saying that they are "butchered" rather than "slaughtered." There's a big difference, especially when you consider the contrast between my description of how I began with the chickens and the assembly line method which is more commonly used.[7])

While it is true that there have been improvements in the way *sh'chitah* is done and that the other methods may not always be any better, it is important to admit that there are still problems that need to be addressed. For example, the way the animals are shackled can cause great *tza'ar ba'alei chayyim* which, as we have already seen, can be grounds for rendering an animal not kosher even if the proper procedures have been observed. There is also a concern for the kind of box into which an animal is guided so that the box doesn't create

---

[7] In addition to the extra degree of separation which assembly line butchering adds between the animal and people, this process also allows for new kinds of cruelty which are at least as painful as shackling without prior stunning. See *Fast Food Nation* by Eric Schlosser (NY; Houghton Mifflin Books, 2001).

gratuitous suffering for the animal at its last moments of life. Even when concern for the animals is not what motivates us, it simply isn't a good thing when you consider what we may be eating when the animal dies in a way which is stressful, such as the adrenalin released into its system because of the fear it is experiencing at the moment of death. It benefits us all if we can make it easier for the animal when it is slaughtered.

Tranquilizing Animals

When I watch TV programs set in the wild, I've seen that they sometimes tranquilize animals by hitting them with a tranquilizer dart. Then they do whatever they need to do, such as fastening a tracking device on the animal or checking its health. It is clear that there is no damage to the animal and, when the tranquilizer wears off, it continues about its life. That leads me to seriously consider the possibility of tranquilizing animals before *sh'chitah*.

I don't yet have a clear answer. Tranquilizing is definitely different than stunning since we know that this will not affect its status as a *bar kayama* and so would not render the animal *treifah*. I would like to see a conversation begin on this question. The starting places would be empirical: What effects might the tranquilizer have on the people who eat the meat? Where is the best place on the animal's body to inject the tranquilizer? Does the tranquilizer concentrate primarily in the blood, which is then drained, and so would have less of an impact on the meat itself? Then we could engage the larger question of whether tranquilizing is harmonious with the rest of halachic reasoning about *sh'chitah*.

Resurfacing Blades

There are other areas of *sh'chitah* where I do believe we could authorize improvements to the classical methods by using currently available technologies. One example is the requirement to hand sharpen a *chalef* to remove a *p'gimah* / flaw or nick. Today, there are ways in which machine made blades could be certified as *chad v'chalak* / sharp and smooth using an electronic inspection. This would allow a *shochet* to kill a number of animals without having to check the blade in between each one. After a certain number of uses, the blade would then be sent back to the factory to be resurfaced and re-certified. This way, the *shochet* can pick up five blades at a time and bring them back for resurfacing after they've been used. In addition, if these blades were made of stainless, surgical steel, then this could really be an improvement in the quality of the *chalef* and therefore in the speed with which the animal dies than some of the *chalafim* / knives in use today.

One more issue with regard to *kashrut*. According to the Talmud, blood which has separated from the limbs and is not contained by the veins and arteries is prohibited, but at a lesser level than the blood of the *nefesh*, or life force, which is drained from the animal by the method of slaughter. Consuming the blood of the *nefesh* carries with it the penalty of *karet* / separation; consuming the blood which separates is a prohibition which, according to some sources, can make the consumer liable to a flogging, but no more.[8] Some sources indicate that blood remaining in the limbs can be removed or prevented from leaving the tissue through a par boiling or marinating process; however, this too is forbidden because we are no longer *baki* / expert in doing this.[9] This raises both the question of whether some form of this process might be made available to us as well as the issue of whether a loss of knowledge of a given process has to be considered permanent.

---

[8] *Karet* is usually understood as a form of capital punishment administered by God rather than a court. It could also be a form of excommunication.

[9] See the *Bet Yosef* on the *Tur, Yoreh De'ah* 67:1 and the *Shulchan Aruch Yoreh De'ah* 73:1-2.

Becoming Baki

Years ago, I wrote an article called "Toward an Empirical Institute for *Halakhah*," which I sent to an Orthodox magazine for publication. In this article, which they chose not to publish, I noted that there are about 35 places in *Yoreh De'ah* where this phrase or a variation of it occurs: *ein anu b'ki'in* / we are not expert. Today, with laboratories and a greater sophistication in testing methods, it is possible to clear up many of these uncertainties and we can again become *baki*. My question was, and is, whether we can then have the courage to make the changes which this new information should allow. [10]

A good example has to do with a blood spot in an egg. If the spot is clearly in the albumen, then one need only remove the spot and the egg is kosher. However, if the spot is close to where the albumen and the yolk meet, then it is unclear whether this is the beginning of a chick which would then render the egg not kosher. The uncertainty derives from a lack of clarity on whether the chick emerges from the albumen or the yolk or from both.[11] As a result, when the spot is in that grey area, the egg is forbidden, which in turn led to the common practice of forbidding any egg which had a spot on it. Now, however, we know for certain that the chick emerges from the albumen and the yolk is its food, meaning that at least in theory we can re-evaluate this prohibition of all eggs with spots.

This example, as well as others I could give, show that in many cases where the later authorities believe that we are no longer *b'ki'im* / expert enough to make fine, but important distinctions, we can use modern tools to rediscover that

---

[10] There is a halachic principle that a ruling from a previous generation can be reversed if we can demonstrate knowledge which was not available at the time the original was made. See Joel Roth, *The Halakhic Process* (1986; The Jewish Theological Seminary), "On New Legal Sources within *Halakhah*."

[11] Just as the rabbis believed that a person is a mixture of the white (semen) of the father and the red (menstrual) blood of the mother.

expertness. To do this, however, means as well that we have to accept that modern techniques and knowledge can be superior to those available to previous generations, which in turn runs counter to much of opinion in the Orthodox world that decisions made by previous generations cannot be overturned. Taking this one step further, it also means that we would need to drop our fear of modernity as the destroyer of Jewish practice and adopt a more collaborative relationship with the present.

Salting/Soaking Alternatives

Let's carry this line of reasoning back to the previous issue of our not being expert enough to use par boiling or a marinating process to remove blood that may be in the limbs and meat of an animal. Today, we are much more aware of the risks to health involved in high sodium intake. By claiming that we are not expert enough to use an alternative to the salting and soaking method of kashering meat, we are requiring people who need to reduce their salt intake and still want to eat kosher meat to ingest all the salt that the meat may have absorbed in the kashering process. If, on the other hand, we work to regain the knowledge of how par boiling or a vinegar marinate can be used to kasher meat as an alternative to soaking and salting, then we can help reduce people's salt intake.

This resistance to change comes from believing that *ein anu b'ki'im*; we no longer know the relationship between the amount of fat on the meat and the required strength of the vinegar and whether boiling is really required and how big a piece it can be. Further, once we have lost this knowledge, it will never again be available nor will anything we learn in the future be able to take its place. But what if using a microwave oven could qualify as broiling? In medicine, diathermy is a way of generating heat which can cause bleeding vessels to clot. The same technique applied to meat would fix the blood in the meat so that it would not flow and thus it would be made kosher in the way that broiling accomplishes the same purpose without requiring additional salting and soaking.

When I first wrote the article suggesting an empirical institute for *halachah*, these were the kinds of questions with which I wanted people who work in the kosher laboratories and those who give all the *hechsherim* / certificates of *kashrut* to concern themselves. My sense is that these and similar questions still exist and need more thought. For instance, could we use Epson salts to kasher meat specifically for people who cannot have sodium salt? What adjustments can we make when a person's health is at stake? Just as I believed then, I still think that some of these issues could be resolved by referring them to labs.

What a Rabbi Needs to Know

Do you remember the joke about the person who wants to know what *b'rachah* to say over his new Jaguar? One rabbi asks back, "What's a *b'rachah*" while the other asks "What's a Jaguar?" Today, we need rabbis who know both what a *b'rachah* is and what a Jaguar is. This is another way of saying that what we need are people who know how *halachah* works and who also understand technology. The kinds of issues I've raised as well as many other possibilities require a conversation between *halachists* and those who know and work with the technologies. We need to encourage the creation of an empirical way of approaching all these *halachot* beyond just dealing with them by text (i.e. precedent) alone.

This need for a better relationship between text and technology applies within *halachah* as well. For example, rather than teaching *hilchot treifut* through text study alone, we could augment the texts with video recordings. When the text talks about *sirchah* / lacerations in the lungs, it could be shown on the video. The same could be true for demonstrating the difference between a normal and diseased liver. This would be more helpful than it might seem at first glance, because today very few Orthodox rabbis have *shimmush* / hands-on experience in these things. They can tell you what the *Ba"ch* and *Pri Mgadim* say, but they also have probably never actually seen what these things look like.[12]

Let me give you an example of a real situation in which this approach of going beyond the text was actually used. A woman came to her *rov*[13] concerned because she found a bit of wheat in her Pesach borscht and wanted to know if she needed to throw it all out.[14] The *rov* asked her to bring him the piece of wheat. When he looked at it, he asked her what she had used to sour the borscht. She replied that she had used lemon. In other words, it wasn't a piece of wheat she had found, but a lemon seed! The rabbi had decided to check out what she had told him by empirical means and so the borscht went from *chametz* and *treif* to kosher by examining exactly with what he was actually dealing. This story shows that it is permissible to employ empirical and experimental methods, where utilizing modern knowledge of how things work would enhance our ability to interpret *halachah* for our time.

---

[12] The *Bach, Bayit Chadash* / A New House, is a commentary on the *Arba'ah Turim* of Rabbi Ya'akov Ben Asher. The *P'ri M'gadim* is a commentary on the *Shulchan Aruch*.

[13] Her rabbi in the sense that he was the one who rendered halachic decisions for the community in which she lived.

[14] On Passover, even the smallest amount of *chametz* / leavening renders the entire dish not kosher. This is called *chametz b-mashe'hu* and is different from ordinary *kashrut* which says that if the proportion is less than one part in sixty, then the mixture remains kosher.

Kashering

Continuing with this train of thought, let's spend a moment talking about kashering for *Pesach*. Not everything can be kashered with heat, but we do know that there are caustic cleansers available (some of which may be more environmentally friendly than others). It would seem to me that if we could identify those which aren't harmful to the environment and use them in solution to soak dishes for twenty-four hours in a bathtub, then any *chametz* that might have adhered to these dishes would dissolve. What I'm saying is that there may be ways to use chemicals in the kashering process that would accomplish what earlier authorities thought was impossible, allowing us to kasher things for *Pesach* which we couldn't kasher before.[15]

From Issur to Hetter

This takes me to the relationship between that which is forbidden (*assur*) and that which is permitted (*muttar*). I've written about this elsewhere,[16] but I want to raise it here as well. How long is an *issur* an *issur*? Can an *issur* / something forbidden mutate, as it were, into a *hetter* / something permitted? For example, if I take a slice of pork and bury it in a big flowerpot in which I then plant an apple tree, are the apples that grow on that tree kosher? They are nourished by the nutrients in the soil which are absorbed by the tree's roots, and many of them are coming from this slice of pork. So, are the apples kosher?

---

[15] This has a social and economic significance as well, since many people today want to live a simpler life with fewer possessions, and needing a full set of extra dishes and pots which are used only one week a year seems an unnecessary extravagance. (ds)

[16] See Renewal is Judaism NOW!, page 70.

We all know that the apples are kosher. But the unasked question is, "What is it that happens between the pig and the kosher apple?" There is a halachic principle that, "*Ein m'vatlin issur l-chat'chila* / One cannot eliminate the forbiddenness of something at the start," you cannot make it disappear.[17] Nevertheless, we live on spaceship earth, and the most special *shmurah matzah* for *Pesach* under *Satmarer hashgachah* has in it some molecules that were once in a porcupine and a skunk.[18] It's all organic matter which is continually being recycled.

Is there a way to identify a point at which we say, "Up to here it is forbidden. Then, when such and such a chemical or physical interaction takes place, the *issur*-ness of that item vanishes and the thing becomes sort of *parve* / inert. After that, depending on what it becomes, it could shift once more and become kosher."

For example, if I take a protein that comes from pork and put it through a process called hydrolysis,[19] then many of the markers which identify it, its "ethnic" components if you will, or its original building blocks, disappear. In a way, all that's left is protein at such a generic level that one can no longer see the chemical markers which identify this protein as pork or another as beef.

My sense is that, when this occurs, namely when we reach the place where the substance can no longer be identified, that

---

[17] See Talmud *Bavli Beitzah* 4b. Using the same example, there is nothing one can do to make a pig kosher. (ds)

[18] *Shmurah matzah* is made from wheat which is guarded against moisture from the time of harvest. Regular *matzah* is made from wheat guarded from the time of grinding. Satmar is generally seen as the most stringent of all Chassidic groups, so Reb Zalman is saying that no matter how carefully one tries to avoid the presence of *treif* within *kosher* it is, theoretically at least, impossible. (ds)

[19] Hydrolyzed Protein is protein that has been broken down into its component amino acids (Wikipedia). It can be found in the list of ingredients of various products.

it would be appropriate to say, "Up to here it is a forbidden substance and when such and such an intervention has happened, the substance no longer is forbidden."

Let's take another basic example. Supposing we take a pot of lard and break it down into its two major components of protein acids and glycerin bases. Once the acids and bases are broken apart, the substance becomes something different than what it was before. A litmus paper test before the chemical change would have been neutral. After the change, it will show red on the amino or protein acids and blue on the glycerides. This makes it pretty clear that the lard was a composite of these two elements and its quality as fat is lost when broken down.

This is another confirmation of my sense that when you break the basic chemical connections, you remove that which created the *issur* and we can start again to determine the potential *kashrut* of what results. However, when I've tried to talk to the people in the field who give *hechsherim*, they haven't wanted to know of these kinds of things.

A similar question to the one posed regarding chemical changes to lard is the question of how long something *milchig* remains *milchig*? Lactic acid (i.e. milk acid) is found in many substances. For example, did you know that when we exercise, our muscles produce lactic acid? There is a little bit of lactic acid in many brands of ginger ale. Can I have a *fleishige* meal with ginger ale that has lactic acid? Should lactic acid be considered *milchig*? Is it *pareve* or perhaps *fleishig*? At which point do we speak about this as no longer having any relationship to milk?

I believe that these are important questions, because they are not just about these products or chemicals. They are really about how we relate to recent additions to our knowledge and the extent to which they influence our willingness to make changes in traditional practice as a result. That's why I feel that these questions need *iyun gadol* / **deep attention**; they need people who will devote themselves to working with them.

Now I want to turn my attention to things which may be controversial in actual practice and not just in theory.

Mikveh

For many years, I was actively interested in helping people have meaningful *mikvehs*, both in terms of the physical structure and the nature of the experience. I want to describe this interest in the form of a true story.

I was about to officiate at the wedding of a couple in California who were part of the House of Love and Prayer which had been established by Rabbi Shlomo Carlebach and others in the late nineteen-sixties. This couple lived in Northern California and, before the wedding, I asked them whether they had immersed in a *mikveh* / **ritual bath**.

The *chossen* / **groom** told me that they had an amazing *mikveh*. A brook ran right through their property, fed by a spring. They had tiled out a basin in one part of the brook so that the water could run into the basin at one end and out the other. They also had a sauna which they had fired up. First, they took dips in the *mikveh* and then spent time in the sauna.

A little later on, at the *chasseneh* / **wedding**, a man came over to me and asked, "Is this not like *Chabad?*" And I said, "Well, in some ways it is and in some ways it isn't; there are some differences." "What's the difference?" he asked. I replied by telling him how the *chossen* had described their *mikveh* and how real a *mikveh* made from a natural stream was to him. If they had really been classical *Chassidim* in the *Chabad* tradition, he would have said, "Well, we don't really have a *mikveh*. We only have a brook and a pool."[20]

I believed then that we needed to create *mikvehs* which were less clinical and more natural, without fluorescent lights and white tiles. Such *mikvehs* would be more like a grotto and entering them would be like entering a mystery where something very special and holy is happening.[21]

I once suggested at a healing center meeting that the center should include a *mikveh* so people could do immersions for the sake of healing. It was Orthodox rabbis who were against this idea. In their minds, the only real purpose of a *mikveh* was for kashering women once a month, and they didn't have a deeper sense of what using a *mikveh* could mean.[22]

Once we can grant how spiritually helpful a *mikveh* can be, it may also be possible to think more creatively about how to set up a *mikveh* under different conditions so that we can make this experience more accessible. I'm thinking in particular of places where there is little rainfall or few natural bodies of water. Could we consider using distilled water for a *mikveh*, for example? Producing distilled water involves a process much like natural rainfall, where the water is boiled (evaporation) and re-

---

[20] Traditionally, a bride and groom each go to the *mikveh* before the wedding (separately). While the idea of what constitutes a "real" *mikveh* began with a natural body of water, over the years it came to mean a pool housed in a building. Thus, a *Chabad Chassid* would see such a *mikveh* as truly real, since it was constructed carefully to fulfill halachic requirements and could be "trusted" more than a natural body of water. This couple, on the other hand, living in a rural location, saw the reality of *mikveh* in the natural body of water and in the spirituality of their experience. (ds)

[21] Reb Zalman's vision is beginning to manifest in new *mikvehs*, such as *Mayyim Hayyim* in Newton, MA.

[22] Rabbinically, a woman goes to the *mikveh* seven days after her period ends so that she and her husband can make love again. In the Chassidic world, men also go to *mikveh*, often more frequently than women, as a way of cleansing themselves from sin and for increased purity. (ds)

condensed by running the steam through coils which cool the water (rain). The water could then drip into an *otzar* / storage pool which would be *gimmel t'fachim al gabey karka* / three handbreaths built into the ground.[23] In other words, it may be possible to build a *mikveh* which fulfills all the requirements of *halachah* using distillation rather than real rainfall.

In general, I think we need to continue concerning ourselves with how to make a *mikveh* in any location and how to make the experience attractive and meaningful. Wherever possible, try to establish a good relationship with the people who have the key to the local *mikveh*, so that they will allow us to use the *mikveh* when needed and to have enough time to create the meaningful experiences we seek for ourselves and others. Then, when we bring *gerim* and *giyorot* / male and female converts to use it, they won't have to rush through and can take the time for reflection and deepening their experience. Also, whether it is for conversions, healings, pre-wedding, or any other reason, the people who want to immerse can bring their close friends, as *s'faradi* women have always done.[24]

In fact, it would be good for western Jews to learn more about the way *s'faradi* women have used the *mikveh*. Not only have they taken more time and gone with friends, they also have included a *chamam* / Turkish bath with a bride before her wedding, where the women share gifts and wisdom, bring fruit, and celebrate. Then, at the great moment of *t'vilah* / immersion, the purification happens while the women who accompanied the bride sing.

In general, then, I think that *mikveh* needs to be extracted from its clinical setting and redesigned so that it serves the spiritual purposes it is meant to serve.

---

[23] The *mikveh* and *otzar* cannot be portable but must be built into the ground and have dimensions that allow for a complete immersion.

[24] Again, this is the standard practice at *Mayyim Hayyim* and the reader who is interested should visit their website or, better, the *mikveh* itself.

Gerut

Mikveh leads into a discussion and re-evaluation of *gerut* / conversion, which is also a part of *Yoreh De'ah*. The rabbis talked more about male converts from whom they expected both *milah* / circumcision and *t'villah* / immersion than about women. What is especially interesting to notice is the sequence, namely that *milah* comes before *t'villah*. According to a basic understanding of *halachah*, this order doesn't make any sense, because until *t'villah* happens, there can be no *chiyuv* of *milah* / no requirement to circumcise.

This apparent reversal of the sequence was noticed by the rabbis of the Talmud when they raised the question of what the status is of a potential convert when there has been a circumcision but no immersion or an immersion but not circumcision.[25] While they agreed that immersion without circumcision does make the person a Jew, they disagree over whether circumcision by itself is enough. What is important here is why it is argued at all that circumcision is sufficient when it is obvious that it shouldn't be.

I think that the reason for switching the order had to do with Christianity. It was very clear what *Yochanan Ha-matbil* / John the Baptist was doing with people. He was offering them the opportunity to immerse in a *mikveh* to become *m'kabel ol malchut shamayim,* / in receipt of the yoke of the heavenly kingdom. He baptized in the kingdom to come, to do a *t'villat t'shuvah* / an immersion of repentance. Later, Paul determined that immersion alone was sufficient and circumcision was not necessary. That, in turn, created a shyness among Jews, a reluctance to do the same.[26]

---

[25] Talmud *Bavli Y'vamot* 46a.

[26] In the end, the rabbis decide that a conversion is incomplete until the person has both been circumcised and immersed.

In a sense, there is a kind of bad faith about this, a suspicion that a person would immerse and then not go through with the circumcision and still claim to be Jewish.[27] To minimize that risk we say, "Let him do the operation first and then there is no other recourse; then we'll know that he really meant it when he said he wanted to become a Jew." In effect, let him pay first and then fill up the car. It's what one does in a situation when one doesn't fully trust the person with whom one is dealing. And the effect is to break up the ritual, because we can't send him to the *mikveh* until he heals. The other way, he would already have been to the *mikveh* and, once we do the *milah*, he is free to recover on his own and without a schedule.

My own experience is that I rarely had to concern myself with the *milah* of adult *gerim*. Most of the time, the men who came to me were already circumcised and what I had to do was *hatafat dam brit* / drawing a drop of blood as a symbolic circumcision to enter into the covenant. Since I did this myself, I was able to say, "First go and dip in the *mikveh* and then we will do the *hatafat dam brit* right afterwards," which is in better harmony with the larger principles of the halachic process.[28]

This possibility opens the door to a complete re-examination of the whole issue of how we relate to *gerim*. So many people have been dissatisfied with the way the process is handled now where the teaching is focused on the externals of Jewish practice, the "hows," with very little sensitivity to the spiritual needs which is often the reason people are drawn to Judaism.

---

[27] It is important to remember that, in the world of the rabbis, circumcision among men was unusual. It therefore constituted an irreversible mark of Jewishness as well as making clear the distinction between a Jew and a Christian. (ds)

[28] Only a Jewish male is required by Divine commandment to be circumcised, so the obligation would only begin after becoming Jewish and therefore after the immersion.

Permeable Membranes

This leads me to another point in this progression. I've discovered that there are people who are very spiritual and who come to Judaism after they have been through some wonderful and powerful spiritual experiences. In these cases, it doesn't seem appropriate to respond to them with the standard response which the tradition requires. In other words, when a person who is pretty high up on the Kohlberg/Fowler scale comes and says, "I want to become a convert," the traditional statement is to say, "In order to become a convert, you have to give up everything that you ever had before; all your religious and familial connections have to be cut, and you are *k-tinok she-nolad damye* / compared to a newborn. That's a wonderful idea, that becoming a Jew is a fresh start, the beginning of a new life. But at the same time, it is also problematic, because it assumes the person must start over with respect to their moral and faith development.

This contradiction shows up in the issue of a *giyoret* who wants to marry a *kohen* / priest. If we say that she is *k'tinok she-nolad*, then why make her ineligible to marry a *kohen* by calling her a *zonah* / harlot?[29] There is a certain unfairness about saying that, on the one hand, she is really reborn and starting over and, on the other, using her (possible) past history to prevent her from marrying a priest. Does this mean that we think every *ger* has to go back to square one, go to the lowest level of the Kohlberg scale, and start all over again by invoking physical reward and punishment as a motivator with someone who, before becoming a Jew, had gone far beyond that level?

To further nuance what may be unique to our time, my sense is that there are many people who feel close to Judaism and Jews, people whom Jean Houston used to call "psycho-semitic." There was a woman I remember who came to the

---

[29] Talmud *Bavli Y'vamot* 61a.

first and second *kallot* / retreats we held. She asked me once whether she should convert and I asked her, "What for?" She was married to a non-Jewish person. Her children were not Jewish. "Why do you want to convert?" She said, "Because I feel I belong." So I said to her, "Take a look: On the level of *p'shat* / basics, on the level of the *guf* / body, you are not Jewish at this point. But in your *ru'ach* / spirit and in your *n'shamah* / soul, and your *chayah* and *y'chidah*,[30] you're very Jewish. You think Jewish; you pray Jewish; you feel Jewish. It's all there. Maybe, at some point later on, it really will be right for you to become fully Jewish, but right now you can do it voluntarily. Why would you need to become a convert?" In other words, on those deep levels, I believed that this person was Jewish already and wouldn't gain anything through conversion.

On the other hand, we find that very often there are people who, on their outer level, in their *guf*, are Jewish. They were born to Jewish parents and celebrated a *bar* or *bat mitzvah*, but on the inside they're Buddhists or Sufis. On the soul level, for whatever reasons, they walk other paths.

Because of both these phenomena, I have started to talk about "hyphenation." Whenever a person commits to the spiritual renewal of Judaism, it almost always carries with it some commitment to practices learned outside of Judaism. In fact, this is true everywhere in the modern religious world. For example, Thomas Merton was clearly a Catholic Taoist. The Catholics once published a book on Christian Yoga and another on Catholic Zen, to cite only two other of many possible examples. In a very important and positive sense, I feel that all of us in Jewish renewal are hyphenated to some extent.

---

[30] There are five levels of soul: *nefesh* / the animation of the body, *ru'ach* / feeling soul, *n'shamah* / thinking soul, *chayah* / the soul of the soul (basic will to live), and *y'chidah* / so absorbed that it has no will, nothing is attracting or repelling, the total absence of any self will.

Given this new reality, why can't we allow somebody who wants to convert to Judaism to be hyphenated just as many of us who were born Jewish are? Why can't people join us and, while accepting the Jewish part as their core practice, still remain loyal to the best of what brought them to Judaism? For example, imagine a woman who has very strong feelings about her commitment to Jesus, the commitment which brought her to spirituality in the first place. She now wants to convert to Judaism. Do we really have to say to her, "You have to give up that connection and start again from the beginning?" Could we say instead, "Are you willing to be *m'kabbelet ol malchut shamayim* / a recipient of the yoke of Divine sovereignty and *ol mitzvot* / the yoke of the commandments and to live a Jewish life and to have dual citizenship?"

Here, then, is yet another place where I feel that we have to do some serious and courageous thinking. Is this possible? Can we allow it? At this point, I would welcome that possibility; I would welcome it with the understanding that the person takes on whatever any *ger* takes on. In other words, the only thing that I would want to not ask a *ger* to say is that they give up those allegiances that brought them to this place. I realize that this is a crucial issue and that there are who will argue that this is not possible. They will say that a person cannot become accepted for conversion unless s/he is willing to give up everything from before.

In some ways, we could take our cue from Jethro, the father in law of Moses who was a Midianite priest. Even though the Torah doesn't say clearly that he opted to join the Israelite people, it does say that he acknowledged the power of God in redeeming them and he was clearly accepted as a valued consultant and friend. He offered sacrifices and shared a meal, "before God," with Moses and Aaron.

For me, this story calls us to do more than lip-service when we say we believe in interfaith bridges. We need to give others true respect and acknowledge that Christians, Muslims, Hindus, Buddhists, and others are not just idolators who really have no part of the truth, but practitioners of deep spiritual paths which have their own unique gifts to share with us and the world.

Now we arrive at the question of under what rubric do we acknowledge this respect. Many will say, "Yes, we can accommodate others under the umbrella of *b'nai no'ach* / children of Noah (who are counted as righteous by observing seven basic commandments). However, when people take the Jewish scriptures seriously, as Muslims and Christians certainly do, they deserve a status higher than *stamm* / just *b'nai no'ach*. Unfortunately, we have convinced ourselves that we cannot have any dealings with other religions. I think, then, that this issue of our inter-faith relationships, of that hyphenation, that bridge, which I call the *ha-mavdil* / that which distinguishes, is very important.

Who is the *Ha-mavdil* / Divider (in the blessing we recite at the end of *Shabbat*)? It is God who is the *Ha-mavdil*, the One who distinguishes *bein kodesh l-chol* / between the holy and the secular, *bein or l-choshech* / between light and dark. It's God who is the interface *bein yisra'el la'amim* / between Israel and the other peoples, between religions. When we understand that the other guys aren't bad or wrong or false or evil, that we can see them respectfully, then this leads to a whole refiguring of the relationship that it is akin to how we create semi-permeable membranes with lots of flow back and forth. The membranes shouldn't be totally permeable, but they also can't be impermeable.

These are the questions that I would like you to think about and then to add your own to my list.

Yoreh De'ah
Appendix: *Eco-Kashrut*
[Edited transcript of talks given on April 1 and April 15, 1998.]

Bella Abzug died on March 31, 1998, the day before the first of these two talks. I dedicated this session to her in recognition of the contribution she made to open us to the idea of femininity and to the real women in the world and their power; their input, and their feistiness.

If I were to ask those women whom we think of as our *bubbies* / grandmothers, "What would you have learned from your grandmother?" I imagine that their responses would be about the right way of doing things. "Come my child and I'll show the right way to peel potatoes. If you cut too much, you're wasting. If you cut too little, then you are asking others to eat the eyes and other flaws which are on the surface." "Come and I will show you how we take a living chicken and turn it into food; how we harvest the meat from this living being. And I'll show you what we do with the blood so that we don't eat what was the living soul of this bird which belongs only to God." This is how a folkway becomes ingrained. People begin to do these things before they articulate reasons for why they do it.

This is contrary to the way people usually talk about what's kosher. When people talk about what is permitted and what the law demands, they speak as if the first step was an idea that there should be something called "kosher." The second step is to decide what is kosher and what is not kosher. But I don't think it really happened in that way. I think we did it first and created the system second.

Think about early human beings and their customs. They were much closer to their instincts than we are and traditions emerged among them by which you were identified as a human being of your clan, your family, and your way. Later, as speech developed and became more complex, people ask the elders why they did things as they did and the elders would respond with reasons. Even later, when writing developed, someone wrote out a list of the things they did and did not eat. My sense is that writing the code, the laundry list, of the birds you can and cannot have, of the fish you can and cannot eat, codifies existing practice, rather than creates it.[31]

I'm beginning this way because most people who speak of religion and revelation think of them as originating in a legal entity known as God, who is top boss and calls the shots. This God came down in a cloud on Mount Sinai and delivered a complete set of 613 commandments, 248 positive and 365 negative, and they have to be done! That's how people usually talk about it, as if they're dealing with legislative law. But what if we are dealing with something which is more like a law of nature? There was no legislature that decided how the law of gravity should operate. The law of gravity is an attitude embedded in the universe in such a basic way that one could say that, on the physical level, the law of gravity is the law of love. Two bodies in space are attracted to each other. Doesn't that sound like love? On that basic physical level, if there are two, let them be in a two-ing relationship with each other.

I believe that what comes through the grandmothers are the forms by which we live life. These are laws; not laws decreed, but laws discovered. The best way I have to say it is that the life on this planet is constantly trying to answer the questions, "Who am I? What works? What doesn't work?" This leads to the assertion that no tradition can continue in its form unless, at least to some significant extent, it is a functional tradition. There is something good built into this path that carries life on.

---

[31] Reb Zalman is hinting at the lists of acceptable and non-acceptable animals given in the Torah, where birds, in particular, are listed only by name and not by criteria, as are animals and fish.

This is why I am still not talking theology. I'm simply observing how it comes about and that it exists in our world. I'm asking the same questions one asks in a laboratory, "What makes it work. If I do this, will it work differently? If I change that, will it work better?" Over time, I discover that certain things work well and they continue being effective for generations. Those that didn't work fell into what people call desuetude – nobody does this any more. Those things are honored by being remembered, though they are no longer relevant. Current practices of a living tradition have function in the present. So if someone says to me, "Reb Zalman, could you tell me what is the reason for this commandment?" s/he is starting at the wrong end. S/he is assuming that the commandment began as legislation, rather than as an empirically successful practice to which reasons are assigned after learning that it works.

Writing the Manual

Once we find out that something works, we can write a manual. It turns out that our sacred scriptures are the first manuals that were written about what things work and why we think they do and it is wonderful that we have them.

There is something else that is really amazing about these manuals. Their language contains fractals. Let me try to explain what I mean by this.

A document like a shopping list or a motorcycle maintenance manual doesn't have fractals. The language used has one meaning at a time. If you take this bolt and fasten it here, then the two pieces will hold together. There is no deeper meaning; it doesn't have fractals. A newspaper doesn't have fractals; a poem does. When there are fractals, then what is "below" is also "above" and the detailed instructions on the physical plane point to corresponding truths on the spiritual. This is what we find in the writings that people have accepted as holy scriptures. It is so in Shruti and in the Koran, as well as in the Bible; wherever people have sacred scripture. Once you open up the meaning and the language, it resonates on many levels at once; it has fractals, many levels of meaning.

When the Torah tells us what's kosher and what's not kosher, it is giving a list of particulars and principles[32] that people have already observed as working. The reasons why we do things in this particular way are the afterthoughts to the experience, what came through to us in the transmission. Why we care about all these details and how we observe them are the theories and stories we create to give coherence to the list and hold all those details together so that we can continue to fulfill the higher purpose of these practices.

Every tradition is located in its own technology. A seafaring people's tradition will be built around the experience of going out in boats, of fishing, and of finding your way on the water. A people of shepherds will have a tradition built around sheep. This is where we Jews originate and it is truly represented in our tradition's technology. Think of how we use a ram's horn, write our Torah scrolls on sheep skins, put on woolen *tallitot* and wear *t'fillin* made from leather of sheep. You could say that this is the genetic material that makes for what is *kosher*, arising from being shepherds and then mixing with the agricultural which may be a somewhat later graft. This is how a tradition gets put together.

Asking the Basic Questions

The technologies of different people create the forms of the fundamental question about meaning, "How do I do what I need to do in a way which is most harmonious with the greater-good of all?" These forms emerge from the processes and

---

[32] Such as cud-chewing and split hoofs for animals and fins and scales for fish.

customs unique to each people. With Jews, as with others, we begin to articulate these questions and answers after the practice becomes entrenched. One approach is to say that we observe *kashrut* because God said this is what is required. It is not necessary to know why because God is smarter than we are and it is enough that we received this practice from God's mouth. God wants this from us because God is wise and knows what is best for each person. God's wisdom goes beyond our ability or need to understand, for "My thoughts are not your thoughts."[33] God's wisdom is beyond mine and my role is to surrender. That's one level of why one might keep kosher.

A second level of response is that a human being can often be capricious and/or selfish. We need discipline in order to be civilized beings. So *kashrut* is necessary because it ennobles us. We practice it not so much because God said so, but because practicing this discipline helps us become more civilized beings.

A third and stronger response says that if a person just grabs food and stuffs it in his/her mouth whenever hungry, then s/he would never think about the larger issues. If, on the other hand, one has to make a blessing over the piece of bread before eating, if one has to say, "*Baruch atah* / Blessed are You, YAH our God, Ruler of the universe, who brings forth the bread from the ground," before eating, then there is a better chance of thinking of the baker, the farmer, the earth – the whole chain of being that is connected with this food and for which one now gives thanks. The argument is that one would not have that consciousness without an "interrupt." A lot of what happens when you view a practice in this way is that the discipline becomes an interrupt to mere animal-like behavior. That interrupt creates a space in which consciousness has a chance to become larger and this is the reason for the practice.

---

[33] Isaiah 55:8; often cited by chassidic rebbes.

Fourth, there are other reasons that refer to energy systems. Some of these are ennobling and refining and others can drag you down, making you heavy and unconscious. Given a choice of which energy system to plug into, I would imagine that most people would prefer the system which is ennobling. For example, suppose the next generation of homes were built with two kinds of electrical outlets. One kind is set up to receive power only from a nuclear generator and the other, a little more expensive, receives its power from a wind generator. Again, given such a choice, I would hope people would choose the wind generated power. There is a similar way of looking at *kashrut* in which the energy source into which one taps when keeping kosher is seen to be cleaner.

This is the approach taken by kabbalists. They talk about an energy system of holiness, *k'dushah*, and an energy system of evil forces that drag things down, called *k'lippah*. In other words, there are the forces of entropy on the one hand and forces that are life enhancing on the other. From which do you want to derive your livelihood? Where do you want to plug in? The kabbalists explained *kashrut* as plugging into the energy system of holiness, or at least into the energy system that can be used for holiness, since the energy of *k'lippah* is very difficult to convert to holiness.

Fifth, there are people who say that the reason for keeping kosher is that it adds a level of dignity both to the food source and to the person consuming the food. There are many *halachot* and customs which do indeed point toward this goal. I remember being taught that when preparing to slaughter an animal, "*Mashkin et ha-b'hemah kodem ha-sh'chitah* / Give the animal a chance to drink its fill beforehand."[34] I've seen people deliver chickens in coops, treating them as merchandise even

---

[34] Reb Zalman learned ritual slaughter when a young man and practiced it for several years as part of his function when he travelled to visit Jews living in out of the way places. (ds)

before they have been dispatched and not as living beings that might be thirsty. So the structure of *mitzvah* is designed to make sure that we treat animals as the living beings they are, right up to the end. Use a knife to cut the throat, going through the carotid artery, the gullet and windpipe in such a way that the brain is immediately deprived of blood and so loses all awareness of sensation. The knife has to be so sharp that it can lift skin when you put it on your finger and so smooth that there is not a single nick. The *shochet*, the one who prepares to slaughter the animal, has to take his fingernail and run it over the edge and back, and feel for the slightest nick. If there is one, he has to keep honing the blade until it's gone. Then the *shochet* says a blessing before slaughtering the animal, thanking God for showing us how to slaughter animals in a way which is holy.

There is a good case to be made that, if we are going to eat meat, then killing the animal must be done with a high degree of consciousness. So this is an approach which adds dignity to both the animal and the person. These principles emerge from the biblical injunctions against killing a mother and its offspring on the same day and chasing away the mother bird before taking eggs from the nest.[35]

Finally, there are also those who say that the basis for *kashrut* is in a compromise. We were meant to be vegetarians and, when we read the first two chapters of the Torah, we see that human beings are only given vegetation as their food. It is after Noah and the flood that the Torah adds meat to the human diet. In this approach, *kashrut* is a compromise between being vegetarian and eating meat indiscriminately. *Kashrut* is as far as one can go to eat meat with a clear conscience. But, being a vegetarian is the ideal.

---

[35] Leviticus 22:28 and Deuteronomy 22:6.

Kashrut and Ethics: The Background

What we have seen thus far is that there is a variety of reasons given for *kashrut*. What they all have in common is that they follow the practice rather than initiate it. Folkways have a dynamic of their own and, in a community where there is continuity, these folkways will travel from generation to generation. Those that are particularly old and entrenched become that way because of their positive relationship to the survival of the community, while those which stop being observed did not serve that purpose as long or as well. At the same time, those reasons which include an ethical dimension also serve the higher purpose of the Jewish people and its survival better than those which rely on simple obedience to a Divine command.

This view is supported by other practices which clearly link food with ethical behavior and where Scripture itself provides reasons. For example, the Book of Ruth tells the story of how Naomi returns to Bethlehem with her daughter-in-law Ruth. When they arrive, they are poor and homeless. To get food, Ruth goes into the fields during the harvest and picks up the grains that the gleaners drop. She can do this because of the *mitzvah* that whatever falls to the ground belongs to the poor.[36] This way, the poor have a right to this part of the harvest, given them by God and independent of charity.

There are other such linkages made between a practice related to food and ethical behavior. Levites receive a tithing from the harvests, in recognition of their spiritual service to the people for which they gave up their share of the land. A basic requirement around eating meat is that one may not cut a limb while the animal is still alive, but must kill the animal first.

---

[36] See Leviticus 23:22 and Deuteronomy 14:28-29. In other places, the Torah speaks of remembering the poor since the Israelites were slaves and poor in Egypt.

Sparing an animal unnecessary suffering is so basic that it is considered one of the seven *mitzvot* given to Noah and his sons after the flood and is independent of *kashrut*.

Returning specifically to *kashrut*, even saying the blessings and using a proper knife are not sufficient. After the slaughter, the *shochet* reaches in with his hands and feels every part of the lungs, the stomach, and the gut to be sure the animal was healthy. If the lungs have adhered to the sides, in other words it was a tubercular animal, then it is not kosher even though the slaughter was done properly. This is only one of a number of such laws about what internal state the animal has to be before it is declared kosher.

Before moving more directly to the idea of eco-*kashrut*, I want to review more of classical rabbinic practice. Once an animal is declared to be kosher, meaning that it has also passed the internal examination, then the meat is soaked in water and salted. This is to fully draw out any blood which may have entered the meat, because the Torah speaks of the blood as the essence of life which belongs only to God.

Another aspect of *kashrut* is the practice of not mixing meat and dairy. This is something which illustrates the power of folkways, since the Torah itself does not explicitly forbid this and so all reasons that are given are after the fact. We really don't know the origin of this practice, but it is so deeply ingrained in us that people have a visceral reaction when they see someone starting to put a dairy spoon into a meat dish.

There are rules about dishes, pots and pans. If, for example, something non-kosher was inadvertently cooked in a kosher pot, then it can't be used it until it has been through a particular kind of purging; only after *kashern* / making kosher, can one use that pot again. And, when one buys something new, it is immersed in a *mikveh* to purify it before use.

From Classical Kosher to Eco-Kosher

In order to have clarity around maintaining *kashrut*, there needs to be clarity around the origin of a product. One reason why manufacturers list ingredients on packages of food is as a response to our needs. They knew that the Jewish market would be closed to them if they didn't post the ingredients, since this lets Jews know whether there are pork or other forbidden products in them. There are also a growing number of kosher "seals of approval." These include the very well-known OU which is modern Orthodox and international, as well as regional certifiers such as MK (Montreal Kosher) and others which are more generic such as a simple K. In some situations, *kashrut* standards are higher than those of the government, which has led many non-Jews to trust a kosher label on tuna when they want to be sure it is dolphin-free and on other products as dairy free when they are lactose intolerant.

Now, we need to expand this discussion beyond the issue of origin to that of outcome, which will also re-connect the practices with ethics. The way I began was to look up the two word phrase, *bal tashchit* / lest you destroy. Originally this law referred to a war; when besieging an enemy town, it is forbidden to cut down the nearby fruit trees.[37] Over time, this specific law was expanded into a more general principle which requires respect for anything that is usable and has value for the world. I remember hearing that every time people cut down a living tree without asking its permission, as it were, the tree screams out and this scream goes from one end of the world to the other. If you think of this in terms of the morphogenetic field of tree-ness, then clear cutting is an outrage over which the trees are crying out in pain.

This leads to an interesting situation of potential conflict. Its humorous side is in the old jokes about Jewish mothers

---

[37] Deuteronomy 20:19.

pushing their children to eat everything on their plates even when they are no longer hungry. In order not to have throw away good food, people are pushed to eat beyond what is good for them. On the serious side, there is a discussion in the Talmud about whether a person can be forced to renounce an oath that would harm his/her body. The answer is yes, and one reason suggested is because the *mitzvah* of *bal taschit* applies to one's own body as well as to living creatures outside that body. In a way, it's too bad that we didn't know how to invoke that conclusion when we were being encouraged to eat too much.[38]

There is precedent, then, to say that there are some rules which are more concerned with effects rather than origins. Another that I think of is the ruling to not eat fish and meat together from the same bowl (even though fish is *parve* and can be eaten at the same meal as meat), but to eat the fish first and then the meat. The rabbis say that to eat them together is dangerous. I don't quite know what the danger is, but my best guess is that it would be easier to get careless and swallow fish bones if one is eating meat at the same time. The same would apply if one eats the meat before the fish, since one may forget to watch for the little bones in the fish. So, it is better to begin with the fish and focus on eating it before moving to something else. Whether I am right or not about the reason is not important, but it is important to notice that *halachah* is concerned about the impact of a practice on the person practicing. Something could be kosher but still forbidden if it might have a harmful effect.

Another way in which we pay attention to the impact of a practice is illustrated by consumer response to Cesar Chavez's organizing of grape pickers. There were enough people who refused to buy non-union grapes to allow the effort to organize and then improve the working conditions of workers to be

---

[38] Talmud *Bavli Bava Kama* 91b.

successful (at least for a time). This corresponds to precedents in *halachah* which forbid buying products produced under extortion or under slave labor, under duress. Even if all the ingredients are kosher, it has an unethical taint which makes it forbidden. Here, the two issues of what it is being used for and what is its origin connect.

Another principle which can applied to *kashrut* is called *mar'it ayin /* the way it looks to the eye, or appearances. For example, it is not permitted to consume the blood of a slaughtered animal, "*Ki ha-dam hu ha-nefesh /* because the blood is the life"[39] of that animal and therefore is to be returned to the ground. Nor can it be left on the surface, but must be covered with ashes or earth. This action has its own blessing, bringing a sense that Mother Earth has to receive this *dam /* blood. *Adamah* is earth, *adom* is red; the earth, the human, and blood are all connected in their root meanings. However, fish blood is not forbidden. So, if one has a bowl with some fish blood in it, then one should leave a fin on the side of the bowl so that it will be clearly visible that this is fish blood and not any other.

Part of *kashrut*, then, demands that practice should be transparent enough that people will not make mistakes when they emulate what they see others do.

Eco-Kashrut

When people began to formulate the gaian hypothesis, they talked about how the earth is alive and that we needed to view the earth as a living being. As we learned more about the environmental impact of our collective behavior as human beings, we extended the principle of *bal tashchit* from individual trees and living beings to whole species and to the planet itself. Issues around the effects of practices and whether they

---

[39] Deuteronomy 12:23.

contributed to the health and healing of the planet hadn't been raised in quite this way before, namely by referring to *kashrut* and other fundamental Jewish *mitzvot*. So I invented the word eco-kosher as a way to identify something as ecologically kosher.

In classical *kashrut*, the best way to be sure that my coffee cup is kosher is for it to be new. Within that system, a styrofoam cup would be the best thing to have. It doesn't conduct the heat, it hasn't been used before, and after I drink from it I can throw it away and nobody else will use it. But what happens when I ask what happens to this cup when I throw it away and I discover that it goes to a landfill where it will sit for many years because it isn't biodegradable? This creates a new kind of decision for someone keeping kosher. When I go to buy my cup of coffee and they ask whether I want it in a "disposable" cup or a mug, what do I do? I don't know what was in the mug before. Maybe something fell into it that wasn't kosher. But that seems like a small consideration in comparison to what happens to the planet when I use disposable cups (and, now especially, the plastic lids). When I choose the mug, it seems that I'm being less strict in my observance of *kashrut*, but at the same time I've become a little more observant of eco-*kashrut*.[40]

These kinds of questions are part of how the current paradigm shift affects Judaism. Continuing in this direction, we need to ask whether the cheapest power is the best power. According to the classical *halachah* of Shabbat observance, we shouldn't adjust anything electric, not even up or down much less on or off. In a traditionally observant household, lights are turned on Friday evening and are left on until Saturday night.

---

[40] Since Reb Zalman first wrote these words, a convergence of these two aspects of *kashrut* happened with the introduction of re-usable mugs which people could bring with them to their favorite coffee shop.

But, viewed through an eco-*kosher* lens. it makes more sense to turn off lights that aren't going to be needed all day.[41]

Eco-*kashrut*, then, is a way of thinking about all the many issues raised by our realization of the degradation we are causing to our environment. Lawn care, water use, pesticides, flying, driving, and shopping are all personal concerns which can be examined using the eco-kosher lens. In a way, the (US) Food and Drug Administration could become a very good agency for *kashrut* supervision, if their oversight were done with more planetary consciousness and understanding of alternative ways of healing and health. Social issues as well, such as the viability of war as an option in international relations, would benefit from an eco-*kashrut* evaluation. Nor is eco-*kashrut* a concern only for Jews. I think we are arriving at a moment where we need to encourage both Jews and everyone else to keep kosher.

---

[41] We realize that this may seem too simplistic to today's readers and it is true that there are other options, including low wattage night lights and timers. At the same time, this can still serve as a useful example of how to formulate current questions and why. (ds)

SHI'UR FOUR: EVEN HA-EZER

Hineh zeh omed achar cotlenu, mashgi'ach min ha-chalonot, metzitz min ha-charakim.
Bati l-gani achoti chalah ariti mori im b'sami...Kol dodi dofek, pitchi li achoti ra'yati.

There he stands behind our wall, gazing through the window, peering through the lattice.
I have come to my garden, my own, my bride; I have plucked my myrrh and spice...
Hark, my beloved knocks! "Let me in, my own..."[1]

Even Ha-Ezer is the section of the *Shulchan Aruch* which deals with relationships, for which *Hilchot Ishut* is the general term used. Freely translated, it means something like, "How to be a *mensch*," how to be a decent human being in the world of relating, whether that is between genders, within an extended family, or in the context of a marriage or other intimate relationship. As always, those involved in the halachic process want to understand this not only philosophically but practically, asking what conduct is most appropriate in specific situations in order to best facilitate becoming the *mensch* to which each person aspires.

Being a Jew Inside

In the previous *shi'ur*, when I was discussing the issues having to do with a *ger*, I talked about how important it is to create a *gerut* of *gam ken yehudi* / **also a Jew**. In other words, how do we create a Jewishness which can acknowledge a person's previous spiritual loyalties while, at the same time, having this

---

[1] Song of Songs 2:9; 5:1-2.

person become fully Jewish? What I didn't talk about is what a person needs to learn in order to become a *ger*.

Imagine that you are a secret agent and you need to be trained to enter a Jewish milieu and act totally Jewish. What would your training entail, so that the way you talked and moved your body would raise no suspicions? One important thing would be to learn what Jews like to eat and how they approach a meal. I remember the Lenny Bruce routine in which he says, "Green Jello is not Jewish. White bread is not Jewish. Corned beef with mayonnaise is not Jewish." In Europe, you would have had to know which Jews break a loaf of bread in half before cutting slices and which cut from the end. In North America, it would be which brand of soda is the most Jewish to order at a deli and when does one need to say the blessing over bread and when some other blessing.

What I would like is to create something like a "charm school" experience for someone who becomes Jewish. When we think of the formal process of becoming Jewish in terms of *halachah*, the rabbis talk mostly in terms of something cognitive, as though becoming Jewish happens because they sprinkle some stuff on your cortex.

And, while study and cognitive learning are important, the limbic is also where you have to be Jewish. This is the place that has to do with ritual, with *kishkes*, the feel. And I want to be clear that this doesn't mean just the way Eastern European Jews express this limbic connection to Jewishness. Rather, there is something about what goes on inside that is really Jewish, regardless of which ethnic branch of the Jewish people one identifies. The people who talk about *gerut* from a purely classical halachic point-of-view, rather than also adding that of Integral Halachah, miss things that have to do with body-language, with how to express feelings, with how one immerses in Jewish music and Jewish books.

It would be interesting to develop resources which people who are in the process of becoming Jewish could use and would also be helpful to Jews by birth in making their Jewishness more meaningful. For example, just as you can buy software to practice for standardized exams, it should be possible to design software and mixed media DVDs that could give a more complete picture of being Jewish than just reading words on a page. While it is important for people to read Buber and Heschel and other inspiring authors, as well as to read the classical "how to" books about being Jewish, it would add so much to have something audio-visual that would show a practice in use, manifesting what it looks like in action.

Anchors of Sacred Relationship

This brings me back to that word *ishut* in its meaning of being in an intimate relationship. Into what does one anchor a committed and sacred relationship? Traditionally, *ishut* / **intimacy** can only happen between two people who are not close relatives already, who are both free to marry, and who are of different genders. In addition, both of them should be Jewish in order for the intimacy to be embraced within the halachic process.

Ishut and Descent

I want to focus on the assumption that "both of them should be Jewish." At this moment, there is a deep difference of opinion between the Reform movement and other branches of Judaism over the issues relating to matrilineal or patrilineal descent. For a long time, halachists have asserted that matrilineal descent is sufficient for the transmission of Judaism through birth, while patrilineal descent is not. Simply put, one is Jewish if one has at least a Jewish mother, but not if one has only a Jewish father.

At first glance, this is an area where *halachah* seems to have gone against its own grain. In everything else, descent seems to be patrilineal. For example, in the famous list of "begats" in the book of Genesis, it says repeatedly, *"va-yoled et…, va-yoled et /* and he gave birth to (i.e., begat) this one, begat this one." This clearly refers to males and a line of transmission which is patrilineal. If we go farther into Genesis (ch. 38), to the stories of Jacob and his sons, we find that Judah leaves his brothers and stays with someone known as *ish adulami /* an adullamite man by the name of *Chira.* There he meets and marries a Canaanite woman, the daughter of someone named *Shu'a.*

There was no question that Judah's sons, *Er, Onan* and *Shela* were considered Jewish, that they were full members of Jacob's extended clan and entitled to inherit their father. If, however, we used later rabbinic acceptance of matrilineal descent only, then they would not have been part of the clan. Nor can we really say that Judah's mother Leah or his grandmother Rebecca "sponsored" Shu'a's daughter at a rabbinic court in Jerusalem, which of course could not have existed at that time, and that this court supervised her conversion to Judaism. It seems obvious that patrilineal descent preceded matrilineal and was in force during the biblical period.

The question is, "Why did we change and accept matrilineal descent as sufficient instead of relying on transmission through the father?" I think it was because our process tends to help the disadvantaged overcome obstacles which are not his/her doing. For instance, such a person could have been the child of a rape by a Roman soldier. The rabbis ruled that such a child had to be reared by its mother, making it a Jew and therefore also the responsibility of the community as a whole. Even though it wasn't implanted with the good will and consent of the mother, nevertheless it was Jewish and to be cared for. It is matrilineal descent that allows for this child to come under the protection and love of the community, as well as that of its own mother. Also, by switching to matrilineal descent during difficult times, at least the community could be sure who was born a Jew, since it may not have been possible to be certain who the father was.

At the same time, I think this choice was an administration of public policy derived not from *ikar ha-halachah* / the essence of *halachah* itself, but rather from a place of a specific concern. Somebody figured that this policy would serve the immediate purpose of fending off disaster, and so enacted what we call a *g'zeirah* / decree in order to protect the integrity of the people as a whole and these particular children, who could then become contributing members of the Jewish people.

The JQ (Jewish Quotient)

I want to propose a different approach for our time, an existential, experiential form of deciding who is Jewish and who isn't. I know that this suggestion can apply to those not born Jewish and seeking entry and I am open to the possibility that it can be used together with or even as a replacement for the older reliance on ethnicity and genetics as the primary determinants of who is a Jew. This approach is built on the assumption that each human being lives in all four of the worlds and is connected to all levels of soul. Given that, I want to be able to identify in which of these worlds and levels of soul a person is mostly Jewish. I referred to this possibility in the previous *shi'ur* in relation to the woman who clearly was Jewish on the upper levels of soul, but not in *p'shat* or in *guf*.

What I'm suggesting is something like a Minnesota multiphasic personality inventory for Jews in which we could ask, "What is your JQ, your Jewish Quotient?" Then, we could all take the JQ test every seven years to check ourselves out. "How am I doing with my Jewish Quotient at this phase of life?" If "normal" were between a given two points and that was the level we were seeking, then we would know when we needed to "add more Jewish to the diet" to build our Jewish quotient! More specifically, we could take a status exam and be able to know which aspects of Judaism we needed to better cultivate.

Using this approach, if a child says, "One of my parents was not Jewish, but I would like to be Jewish by inheritance and not have to go to the *mikveh*," then we would determine whether this person was entitled to be a Jew by measuring his/her JQ. In many ways, this would be a more accurate way to determine Jewishness. From a genetic point of view, half of the genes, the chromosomes, come from each parent. There are no grounds for saying that the half that comes from the mother is necessarily more Jewish than the half that comes from the father, or even that one set of genes is Jewish and the other is not. Biologically, it is neither all matrilineal nor all patrilineal; it is parent-lineal. That's how it really works.

I think it is important to start saying that it is the way a person lives that determines if s/he is a Jew. In this way, we also soften what is often seen as a sharp divide between Jew and non-Jew. We can then make real the way that Rabbi Arthur Waskow speaks of the *tzitzit* / fringes which hang from the edges of a garment and blur the division between the garment and what is beyond it. Looking at being Jewish behaviorally, we can then allow for that domain in between where there is an overflow between religions as well as being a meeting place for them. We would no longer have to invest so much energy in identifying where the line is drawn that encloses our religion and protects it from contamination by others. Rather, we could now point to the no-man's land in between where exchange and sharing can take place.

Returning to the person with one Jewish parent who wants to claim Jewishness as an inheritance, we would evaluate his/her JQ check-up and be able to say, "From here to here it is still iffy whether or not you are Jewish. So, if you want to be counted as fully Jewish, then you'll have to up your quotient. Please come back in half a year when you've upped your quotient and then I'll marry you as a Jew."

This would be an empirically based approach, requiring constant attention and adjustment, rather than a policy based approach. For the most part, I think that creating policy really serves the purpose of helping people avoid having to think. An empirical approach lets those involved in the decision making process be freer, more aware of a range of options and choices, and encourages them to be better prepared. A policy tries to define boundaries in such a way that most cases easily fall into the categories of definitely yes or no. However, that means that those who don't quite fit into the preset categories get evaluated not so much as to who they are but which category they mostly resemble. What is really happening is that people who don't easily fit into the preset categories have characteristics which encourage us to look at them uniquely. Using an empirical approach makes us look at every person that way, not just those who don't neatly fit, and is the better way of working with those who seek to identify themselves as Jews.

Marriage Contracts

This brings me to something that I've been thinking about for a long time and really wishing that people would put into practice. When a couple marries, it is important to have a *sh'tar* / document which creates a mechanism for preventing potential problems down the road. We have a model for this in the traditional *sh'tar t'na'im rishonim* / document agreed to by both sides which spells out under what financial conditions and the time and place of the wedding. What I have created in consultation with halachic authorities is a *sh'tar t'na'ei kiddushin u-nisu'in* which takes into consideration the following items.

Non Compos Mentis

What are the kinds of clauses that I think should be included in a *sh'tar* of this kind for our time? First, if one of the partners is no longer *compos mentis*, then we say that they do not need to stay married, even though the partner who has become ill is no longer capable of agreeing to the divorce. For example, a fifty year old woman married to a sixty-five year old husband who has early onset Alzheimer's is with someone who is physically healthy and may go on living for a long time. However, in effect, this woman is already a widow. Should she be tied to him forever?

Agunah

The issues that have to do with *agunah* have troubled halachists for centuries.[2] I don't know what can be done to help such women after the fact, since this is not my area of competence. However, setting modern *t'na'im* that cover modern issues would serve as preventative measures that can spare a woman from the possibility of becoming an *agunah*.

The classic case of an *agunah* is when the husband is lost in an accident. No one knows for sure what happened, the body hasn't been found, and a number of years have gone by. Instead of leaving this woman "anchored" to the husband, it would be better to write a clause in the *t'na'im* that he would never have agreed to marry her if he thought this would happen and so the marriage is *batel* / null and void if he disappears. Another example would be in a case where half a

---

[2] An *agunah*, or anchored woman, is a wife whose husband has either disappeared without divorcing her or who refuses to divorce her. Since divorce in classical Jewish law must be initiated by the husband, these women are "anchored" to their husbands against their wills.

year has gone by after the civil divorce and one of the partners still refuses to either give or receive a *get* / Jewish divorce. In such a situation, a document they had signed before getting married would have specified that this kind of vindictive behavior renders the original betrothal *batel*.

A document which sets conditions in advance that can nullify an agreement later has a precedent in tradition. The *Rambam* discusses both conditional betrothal and divorce and sets out four requirements which must be met in order for a conditional document to be valid. These are: (1) the conditions have to be phrased both in terms of what will and what will not happen; (2) the positive precedes the negative; (3) the condition must be met before the action is complete; and (4) the condition has to be possible. All four of these principles are derived from the conditional agreement into which Moses and the Israelites enter with the tribes of Reuben and Gad.[3]

Y'vamot

Another place where a conditional, pre-marital agreement could be helpful is to avoid issues around a *y'vamah*. This occurs when a husband dies childless and the husband's brother is required by the Torah to marry the widow.[4] The child of this union is named as the child of the deceased. If the brother is unwilling to marry his sister-in-law, he may perform the ceremony of *chalitzah*, where she removes his shoe and spits on his foot, freeing her to marry whomever she wants. In rabbinic law, *chalitzah* became required, since it is assumed that the widow should choose her next husband and neither party really wants to observe *yibum*.

---

[3] Maimonides *Hilchot Ishut* 6 which is derived from Talmud *Bavli Gittin* 75a and based on Numbers Chapter 32.

[4] While there are stories in *Tanach* which suggest that this requirement extended to other relatives of the deceased as well, the Torah only mandates this marriage when there is a brother. (Deuteronomy 25:5ff)

However, it is still possible that the brother could refuse to participate in the *chalitzah* unless he gets something he wants, such as a larger share of his brother's inheritance. Again, a pre-nuptial document which specified that such behavior on the part of the brother would invalidate the marriage from the beginning would be helpful in preventing additional suffering imposed on the widow.

Begetting With Another

It's also possible to write a clause into the *t'na'im* that if either partner begets a child outside the marriage, the *kiddushin* themselves are *batel*. When I've written such a clause, I framed it so that it applied to either the husband or the wife, even though classical *halachah* could accept his child (if the mother weren't married), but not hers (who would be a *mamzer* / bastard). I wrote this as egalitarian because the sacred and committed connection and relationship that the two of them were establishing would have been broken irrespective of who committed the infidelity.

Loss of Trust

In all the *chassidishe s'forim* / chassidic books, they talk frequently about something called *tikkun ha-brit* / repairing the covenant. What they mean are the drops of semen that were "lost" in youth, prior to marriage, as well as involuntary emissions at any time. I would like to expand the definition of *tikkun ha-brit* to include that which is needed to rebuild trust between people.

Rebuilding trust in a deep relationship where it has been lost is one of the harder things to do in life. One really needs help *min ha-shamayim* / from heaven and a willingness from the people involved to say that we're going to make a new start and we really want to rebuild trust between us. The community to which the couple belongs also has a role to play in this process. A breaking of the covenant of trust is like having a disease which requires major surgery to remove it. There is time needed to allow for healing, during which the community can be supportive just as people might bring food to the home of a person recovering from surgery. Once the immediate healing has taken place, there is also a need to look more deeply into the causes of the loss of trust where, again, the support of others in the form of therapists and friends is crucial to help the couple look at the issues which caused the break.

At the same time, we can also recognize that it can get to a point where, if trust has been so deeply broken, then one would say "the *kiddushin* never were intended to be valid under such conditions and are *batel.*" So, again, it should be possible to write a clause covering this eventuality into the *t'na'im* before the wedding.

Practical Steps

I urge all of you reading this, whether you are a *kli kodesh* / holy vessel who officiates at weddings or if you are planning one for yourselves or relatives, that you seriously consider using ritual and *t'na'im* as ways of building trust and anticipating future eventualities.

Ritually, I find that the *badeken* can be a powerful experience for both families at a wedding. Traditionally, this is the moment when the groom enters the room where the bride is before the ceremony and, after looking at her, lowers her veil. Since this is a moment when the bride is blessed, it is an opportunity for all the members of the families to offer each other both blessings and forgiveness. The wedding day is a personal Yom Kippur for the couple, which is why they fast until after the ceremony, and it presents a wonderful moment for everyone to let go of the difficulties which may have been experienced on the way to the wedding and to begin this new phase with a clean slate. It is, then, one way of helping to build trust through forgiveness and blessing.

Creating *t'na'im* that include the examples I've already given as well as other possibilities that seem real to you is a practical tool for anticipating and dealing with possible difficulties in the future. Members of Ohalah: The Association of Rabbis for Jewish Renewal have access to the templates I designed for this purpose as well as to those done by others. While I realize that writing *t'na'im*, conditions under which the marriage never took place, may seem difficult and anachronous at a moment when a couple is planning a wedding, I have never had a couple fail to agree to *t'na'im* once they understood. They all said, "I love you so much, I care for you so much, that if I were to turn out to be such an S.O.B. later on down the pike, I swear off this marriage at this moment." Helping a couple think of these things can also serve to enhance trust at the beginning and relax possible anxieties that one or the other may be experiencing. My own experience as a rabbi has confirmed the value of writing these kinds of conditional documents.

Divorce Contracts

Years ago, when I was working on my doctorate at Hebrew Union College (HUC) in Cincinnati, I was friends with Professor Jakob Petuchowski of blessed memory. He was a true *lamden / learned* man and I had a very warm and close relationship with him. He was very helpful to me, encouraging me to come to HUC to earn my doctorate, and promising that they would honor my choice of subjects. This was actually quite amazing for that time, since I wanted to write about *Kabbalah* and *Chassidut* which I don't think I could have done at the Jewish Theological Seminary (Conservative) or even at Yeshivah University (Orthodox).

I asked Professor Petuchowski what he thought of the Reform position on divorce as expressed in its 1869 rejection of the need for a *get*. Instead, the Reform rabbis of the time invoked the principle of *dina d-malchuta dina* / the law of the land is the law to declare that a civil divorce was sufficient to allow re-marriage without the risk of *mamzerut*.[5] He responded by saying that he wasn't happy with this decision and would rather see the Reform movement require a *get*. When I followed by asking, "So why not have a *get*?" he said, "Because right now, every time you talk about a *get*, a Reform or Conservative Rabbi has to disqualify himself and send the couple to an Orthodox Rabbi. And, of course, no rabbi wants to do this to him/herself. *Ein adam meisim atzmo rasha* / A person doesn't make himself evil.[6] "I'm a rabbi, but I can't help you; you have to go to the Orthodox rabbi."

I know that any *get* issued by liberal rabbis would, *l-chat'chila* / from the start (i.e. in principle), not be accepted by Orthodox rabbis. At the same time, I am sure that a child born to a mother who remarried after receiving such a *get*, who comes to an Orthodox Rabbi twenty five years later, would not be declared a *mamzeret*. If she presented the papers that prove that a *get d-oraita* / divorce which satisfies the minimum requirements of the Torah was issued, I can't believe that any rabbi would want to take it upon himself to declare her a *mamzeret*, with all the suffering that this would entail.[7]

---

[5] This talmudic principle is usually limited to cases where, though different, the prevailing civil law doesn't contradict Jewish law. It is most often applied in commercial and civil law. While many Reform rabbis today will encourage a couple to seek a Jewish divorce for social and spiritual reasons, they don't require it.

[6] Talmud *Bavli K'tubot* 18b. Meaning here that no liberal rabbi will agree to a situation in which s/he has to admit to being less than a "real" rabbi.

[7] Most traditional authorities will go to great lengths to avoid having to label a person as a *mamzer*.

The reason why both of us cared about the need for a liberal *get* is that we worried about *pilug* / split, the splitting apart that's already happening between Orthodox and liberal Jews, where the Orthodox increasingly feel that they cannot accept somebody whose *yichus* / lineage isn't clear. They are concerned that someone coming to them from the outside may be a *mamzer* or a *sh'tuki* / someone whose father isn't known and so don't want their children to marry them. It's getting to the point where people have to prove their genealogy before a rabbi will marry them and, even with such proof, how can one be sure?

Get D-Oraita

So what we wanted to do was to prevent this *pilug*, this schism in Judaism, from getting any worse. We asked ourselves whether we could come up with a *get* that liberal rabbis could require and which, at least *b-di'avad* / after the fact, be acceptable to Orthodox rabbis. We did design such a *get* and, again, members of Ohalah have access to that document to use as is or modify within its parameters. The guiding principle of this *get* is that it should be valid *d-oraita*, meaning that it should fulfill the conditions spelled out in the Torah.[8]

The husband first writes this *get d-oraita* himself, penciled in, and in English. The reason why the *get* was done in Aramaic was that it should be in the vernacular; that's why we do it in English. The husband sits down, *v-chatav lah* / and he first writes her an affirmation that he wants to give this *get*: "I shall intend, in writing the *get*, to write it in my name, for my wife's name and with the intention that it may be a valid instrument according to the laws of Moses and Israel therewith to divorce my wife that she may marry anyone she pleases." So we begin with a procedure to establish intent and willingness. Then he

---

[8] Deuteronomy 24:1-4.

writes out the *get* in twelve lines. Today, with computers, you can show him how much has to go on each line and you can even get the paper ready for him so that he can trace the lettering by hand.

Once he has written the *get*, it is signed by two witnesses who consider themselves to be *shomrei Shabbat* / **Sabbath observers** by their own definition. I don't want the definition of *Shabbat* observance to come from outside these people and I do want to respect their ways of keeping *Shabbat* and to take their word. The *get* is then given to the woman using the proper rabbinic formula.

Woman's Counter-Get

While the husband writes the *get* mandated by Torah, the woman also writes a counter *get* of her own. This is one way to try and equalize the procedure, since biblical law allows only for the husband to divorce a wife and not the other way around. Her counter *get* allows her to actively disconnect from her husband, rather than just being the passive recipient of his action.

When both documents have been completed, the presiding rabbi says, "You are free to marry anyone."

Karmic Release

At that point, when we have completed the basic procedures mandated by biblical and rabbinic law, we can create an experience of karmic release. One way to do this is to have each member of the divorcing couple write a letter of truth to the other. Once they have been exchanged and read, the rabbi takes them back and burns them, so that they cannot be used later in any way.

If we really believe in reincarnation, then we should also be able to say *hareini mochel* / behold I forgive. I think that it is important for each person to say this formula to the other before giving the *get*.[9] Then, both the giving and the receiving are from a "clean" place, i.e., not from vindictiveness. My sense is that karmic release is really important; to say, "Listen. We didn't do so well this time around and it wasn't meant for our marriage to continue forever. So *gei such gesunder het* / go in health. Live your life and let's hope that the compulsion we needed to fulfill with each other be removed from the karmic wheel, so that neither of us will have to repeat this one."

Next, we complete the process. Each hands the other the *get* s/he wrote. Both of them can leave the room through separate doors and then return. The *gittin* are read again and perforated. A document describing what happened is written and each person receives a copy.

This procedure does not require the involvement of an Orthodox rabbi. At the same time, all the documents are clear and specify the intent of the husband to issue a divorce, the knowledge of the witnesses that they are witnessing a divorce, and the consent of the wife to receive (and give) the divorce. In addition, since the counter-*get* is not required by biblical or rabbinic law, I feel that the witnesses to this *get* written by the wife should be women. I believe that this *get d-oraita* will help everyone feel that they have done the right thing in a conscious and holy way while still remaining true to the intent of the tradition.

---

[9] This formula can be found at the beginning of the bedtime *sh'ma* in *chassidic siddurim* and before *Kol Nidre* in some *ashkenazic machzorim*.

Other Issues in Gittin: Toref

There are some other issues in relation to the *halachah* of *gittin* that I feel we also need to cover. We need to start looking at the *toref* / lines on a *get* that have to be written with precise accuracy. What goes on these lines includes the exact names of both spouses, the name of the place(s) where they live, the date, and other identifying items which cannot be part of a standard template.

I've come to the conclusion that these items should not be written out by the old method, which identifies the place by the rivers that meet there. Today, for example, we would have to write, in Hebrew letters, "in the city of Philadelphia which is on *nahar* / the river Schuykill." Or, if we were in a city which is not on a river or at a confluence of rivers, we would have to identify it by nearby springs or lakes. To meet the standards of precision required by rabbinic law, we need a standardized spelling for all of these English words and terms in Hebrew characters and, in theory at least, if someone spelled any of these words incorrectly, it could invalidate the *get*. Frankfort, Germany was spelled in an awkward way because they wanted to be sure that the Hebrew letter *pei* wasn't used, since it could lead someone to read the city name as "Prankpurt."[10] And even if one thought this was acceptable, how do you make the difference between "Morris" and "Maurice" clear?

If the whole point of the *toref* is to make it person-specific, then we now have other ways, such as using social security numbers. And, if the other purpose of *toref* is to make identifications precise so that they cannot be misinterpreted later and used to invalidate the *get*, then even when we are doing a true rabbinic *get*, we should spell out the names of

---

[10] And so it was spelled, *vav-vav-resh-aleph-nun-kuf-vav-vav-alef-vav-resh-tet* (ווראנקוואָרט).

American places in English characters according to the spelling everyone knows.

Most Jews in North America are bilingual today in the sense that they can read both the English and Hebrew alphabets. In a time when most Jews only read the Hebrew alphabet no matter where they lived, it was different. In those days, Jews wrote German in Hebrew characters (i.e. Yiddish) and so it made sense to spell out German place names in Hebrew letters. Living as we do with full access to a secular school system and integration into this society, the requirements of clarity and precision in a *get* are better met by using the English alphabet for place names and nicknames as well.

There is some support for this in the tradition. The Talmud discusses the status of documents drawn up in non-Jewish courts, written in their languages, and even witnessed by non-Jews. While the majority of rabbis will not accept such a document for the purpose of divorce, Rabbi *Shim'on* does, especially in cases where there may be no Jews to witness. In addition, there is mention made of documents written in one language and signed by witnesses in another. In general, there is a strong case made for leniency when it comes to the way in which *gittin* are witnessed and even read, since *Rabban Shim'on ben Gamli'el* argues that the purpose is to prevent Jewish women from becoming *agunot*.[11] It's really important, now that we have two languages available, to use them in the service of the higher principle of making it easier for a woman to avoid becoming an *agunah* or giving birth to a child who will then be labeled a *mamzer*.

Returning to the issue of place identification, in addition to gaining precision by using English letters for the names, we can now use global conventions rather than local geography to make clear where the *get* is being issued. We can state which

---

[11] Talmud *Bavli Gittin* 10b, 11a, and 19b.

time zone in relation to Greenwich mean time the city is and we can use latitude and longitude to place the city accurately and unambiguously.

These are some changes I want to propose to people who are doing *gittin* in the classical form. I believe them to be appropriate not only because they enhance the precision which has always been a requirement of the rabbinic tradition but also because they help serve the higher purpose of making *gittin* accessible so that people don't become frustrated and decide to ignore the process altogether.

Co-parenting Agreements

Finally, I want to mention that having co-parenting agreements as part of *gittin* is of utmost importance. We need to make clear that what is being severed is the spousal relationship only. The co-parenting relationship continues when there are children of whatever ages and we need to give more thought as to how to speak of this as part of the experience of *gittin*.

Marriage-Lite (Temporary Agreements)

I also want us to learn to talk about agreements to live together for limited amounts of time. It seems clear that, both in our Jewish Renewal communities and in the larger Jewish and general societies, we have accepted that people can care for one another, have a sacred and committed relationship, and live together without getting married. In the past, we called the woman in such a relationship a *pilegesh*.

Today, the concept of being a *pilegesh* / concubine carries negative connotations. It's like she is a "kept woman," even if that were neither its original intention nor a good definition for the relationship as it has evolved. By whatever name it might be called, however, it is clear that this kind of relationship is increasingly recognized in the secular courts and, when the relationship ends, one or both partners can be required to pay what is commonly called "palimony."

There is a parallel in *halachah* as well. When two people have lived together openly and clearly been *shutafim* / partners with one another, then a *get* is required to end the relationship even if they never were married according to Jewish law.

When it is clear that a couple wants to live together but do not intend to have a child, then I think we should be open to exploring agreements that recognize and acknowledge the commitments they are willing to make. Such an agreement may begin with words like, "This couple wants to live together for the next seven years. They have no intent to beget a child...." This is in harmony with an idea I've learned from anthropologists that there are two levels of marriage. One is when you don't intend to beget a child and you make a contract for as long as you wish to make it for. At the end of the specified time, the couple can decide whether they wish to extend their contract or not. The other is when there is an intent to have a child, which requires a contract that takes co-parenting into account and needs to be more open-ended.

I think these possibilities need to be looked at directly and openly both by couples and by the people counseling them.

Homosexuality

I want to say something about what the Torah really says about homosexuality. I know that this has been troubling many people and, even though we have been now been talking about this for many years, it is still important to say it again here.

What the Torah says is, "*V-et zachar lo tishkav mishk'vei isha* / With a male you are not to lie as with a woman, it is an abomination!"[12] Most people have seen in this verse a

---

[12] Leviticus 18:22. See also Leviticus 20:13 where the penalty is death.

prohibition of sex between two people of the same gender who are in a loving relationship. Thus, the intent of Torah seems to be a blanket prohibition of homosexuality, which in turn leads to the whole analysis of homosexuality as a choice people make to consciously rebel against the Divine will.

While I know that this is the way most of the Jewish tradition has looked at this issue and that much of the *halachah* of personal relationships assumes this understanding, I propose that we look for another way of hearing this *passuk* / verse.

What I hear is illustrated by the following example: Men get horny in the single sex prison environment. When a new person comes in, he becomes the closest thing to a woman that they can get, so they engage in forced sex with him. But they really want a woman. In other words, they want *mishkivei isha*, not *mishkivei ish*, but they will take advantage of another male because there are no women with whom they can relate. According to this understanding, the verse forbids straight men from having homosexual sex as a substitute for heterosexual sex and which actually is often the rape of one man by another. The verse is not really saying anything about consensual sex between two gay men.[13]

While I realize that this interpretation of the verse raises issues of its own which require more discussion, I do think it is an interpretation that needs to be explored. If we begin from this more open understanding of the the meaning of the verse, what happens? How does it feel to us and to what extent is it a good beginning for a different approach to gay relationships and marriage?

---

[13] The Torah never explicitly forbids sexual intimacy between two women. However, Reb Zalman does extend this same principle of interpretation to sexual relationships between women. (ds)

We have been taking it for granted that people who are attracted to others of the same gender and who can't feel fulfillment except with people of same gender are still included in that *passuk*. What I'm suggesting as a new starting place is that people with these attractions are in effect saying, "*Iy efshi /* I can't do it any other way." *Iy efshi* means that we are dealing with something that is integral to a person. While the court is still in session over whether being gay is genetic or learned, what I want to say is that people who want *mishkivei ish*, (as opposed to people who really want *mishkivei isha* but who get it from another male), are not included in that *passuk*.

Same Sex Marriage

This leads directly to the question of *ishut bein zug shel chad minim /* marriage between people of the same-gender. How could such a relationship be called *ishut*? I have to admit that I'm not sure. My sense is that we won't know until we live in a society with same sex marriage for a while and see how it works out. I think it will be determined by socio-dynamic and sociological data, the accumulated experiences of committed couples, and by observation. I still have a feeling that *ishut* is connected with procreation or at least with the intent to have a child, in a similar way to what I proposed with heterosexual relationships a little earlier. If a lesbian or gay male couple agrees to bear a child so that you now have, besides their relationship as a couple, a co-parenting relationship, does that bring their relationship closer to *ishut* as it has been classically defined?[14]

Yibum and Surrogate Parenting

Another, and positive way to look at *yibum /* levirate marriage would be in the context of surrogate parenting. I

---

[14] See *Same Sex Kidushin v-Nisu'in* by Rabbi Eyal Levinson (ALEPH ReSources Catalog).

wonder what we might think if a man who was a good friend of the deceased would want, together with the [childless] widow and of course with her consent, to leave her with his child who could then be named for and considered the offspring of his friend, the departed husband. Suppose he were to say, "I want you to have this gift. I will be a donor for the sake of the love that you had for my friend and so that his memory will live on. While we don't want to marry or even fully co-parent, I may, within certain defined limits, participate in the rearing of that child."

Summary

I think that these are the kinds of questions that need to be thought through today. I hope that you will find ways to continue and deepen this discussion so that our Judaism, which has been so precious and so relevant, will continue to be both as we move deeper into this new and uncharted period.

I do want to warn us all against being casual about the issue of *mamzerut*. Remember that in cases of personal status, we have a responsibility to consider *klal yisra'el* / the entirety of Israel, including those who disagree strongly with us. Whatever we do must be done so that we do not have to overcome an immune response over the next few generations when our children and Orthodox children want to marry each other. Think carefully about the responsibility this places on all of us and may all our deliberations and *takkanot* keep this concern in mind.

Even Ha-Ezer
Appendix: Modern Covenants Need A Modern *Ketubah*

(Introductory note: In the preceding chapter, Reb Zalman focused his attention on pre-marital agreements and divorce documents. The following essay deals more with reasons for considering adjustments to the concept of marriage reflected in the traditional *k'tubah* / marriage contract. He wrote this over 30 years ago and it is interesting to note his halachic reasoning, his suggestions for change, and the extent to which his suggestions have grown into a diverse collection of *k'tubot* and wedding ceremonies. The essay is reprinted here exactly as it appeared originally.)

Be my wife according to the Law of Moses and of Israel and I shall work, cherish, feed and support you...And all the dowry she brought...all this the groom guaranteed a hundred zuzim...The responsibility for fulfilling this contract of ketubah, dower and addition I accept on myself and heirs to pay from the very best of my possessions...to be collected even from the shirt on my back. This is not a lean-to or mere legal formula...it is all legal and valid. (from the ketubah)

"Here, you are consecrated to me with this ring *according to the Law of Moses and Israel.*"

This still is the formula we use at weddings and it creates real problems. How honest are the bride and groom and the officiant when they employ this formula? When the rabbi writes out the *ketubah* and gets the witnesses to sign, who cares about the real stipulations of this document? The Talmud tells us that every one who consecrates a wife with *Qiddushin* (the formal act of Jewish marriage) does so according to the opinion of the rabbis. Which rabbis? What opinions?

The intention of the law was once quite clear! The bride and groom contract to live by the laws of the Torah as all the rabbis defined them. Even the shirt on the groom's back was indentured to the bride to live with her in truth "according to the *Halakhot* of Jewish men." The *ketubah* (the marriage contract) guaranteed for a virgin the scriptural 100 *Zuzim* as well as additional benefits in return for the usufruct of her dowry. No Jewish woman need be destitute at the termination of a marriage either by the death of the husband or by divorce.

The Irrelevance of the Ketubah

This protection was once really necessary. Nowadays secular agencies protect a wife through laws of alimony and inheritance. More crucial yet is the fact that none of the participants in the wedding really intends to do what he affirms in writing. The intent of the couple is often romantic and secular. The intent of the rabbi is liturgical and legal in terms defined by the registry of vital statistics which allow him to proclaim "by the authority vested in me...by the State of...I hereby declare you to be husband and wife." Would we not be better off if we were *not* to serve as officials of the state (unless the couple specifically asked us to act as agents of the state)?

A colleague asked me to help him draw up a *ketubah* for a student couple in which their real concerns would be safeguarded. Despite the fact that the traditional *ketubah* was intended to be a real document and not a mere "lean-to or legal formula" we constantly force a shoe on the couple that does not fit. I was not successful. I found no way to include the factual conditions the couple wished to include.

A Jewish Alternative to Marriage

We were faced by the usual dead alternatives. Write a formal *ketubah* and then, in another document, draw up the conditions they requested. But which one is the REAL *ketubah*? One *ketubah* must by necessity void the other. If *Qinyan* (a juridic act of transfer) were to be concluded on the instrument the couple demanded, the traditional one would be pretense. Since brides and grooms prefer to have their relationship covenanted and stipulated according to norms of their own, what ought to be the rabbi's function if he truly recognizes the right of individuals to determine for themselves who they are, what they want to be, and how they wish to relate to one another? How should he act if he does not want to impose *Halakhah* upon people who are really not prepared to live their own lives according to its implication?

Perhaps the only legal tool that he has at present is the concept of concubine, which has fallen into desuetude. Maimonides maintains that concubinage can only be practiced by the King. Still, Nahmanides differs with him. (However, he warns that it might lead to all kinds of transgressions and lewd behavior.) One might nowadays have to revert to Nahmanides' option, since we already live with the problem. *Huppah and Qiddushin* for many involve serious breaches of faith, penalties and problems for the children and those whom the children marry. In our time the very term concubinage has pejorative connotations. Perhaps in time we will be able to educate people to the real demands of marriage *k'dat Moshe v'yisrael.*

A category like concubinage would free us paradoxically to treat the couple like *menschen* again. We could offer the legal structures of *Halakhah* as well as of common law. In drawing up conditions for a real contract a rabbi could have an enormous opportunity to help the couple focus on the values and realities of their new life.

A New Role for the Rabbi

Alternate life styles can be accommodated in common law in ways that the sacred law does not and cannot provide. I am as much for the preservation of *Taharat Hamishpahah* (family purity) in all its meanings as I am for the recognition of contracts and covenants that are real. People ought to have the right to enter covenantal relationships on the basis of real consent. The anxious will only see two alternatives, where I propose three viable and acceptable ones against one unacceptable one, that of random promiscuity. Where there had been no third alternative between the declared holy and the declared vile we could offer a third alternative of human and potentially holy (or even, God forbid, consensual) marriage.

I propose a very serious new look at the role of the rabbi as he officiates in marriages, toward giving couples as many options as possible, allowing them to choose *Huppah and Qiddushin* with all that entails, or to choose other forms of mutual covenanting which truly correspond to their wishes and needs. The latter would require premarital counseling in the rabbi's study that would seriously come to grips with the willingness and ability of the two partners to covenant, as well as with the proper status of women. The reading of a real *ketubah* under the *Huppah* would have a far greater ability to sensitize those who attend the wedding with the intention of the couple whose marriage they have come to celebrate. By assuming a true civil character for the contract in the study the rabbi could function far better in the liturgical realm, planning and reading the kind of service that would be most profound to the bride and groom, and most instructive to the holy community.

R' Yaakov Yosef of Polenoe reports (in "L'shon Hasidim," 287):
I heard in my Master's name (The "Besh't") that from heaven it was revealed to him why "Mashiah" tarries so long! Because they don't take enough time for the great love in the mystery of Kisses which are to precede pairing. For one needs to rouse her desire — if one may be permitted to speak of this — so that she might first come to sow the seed. Thus only is a male child conceived, for this only is compassion. Oh how gracious is the teaching of a wise one!

Originally printed in Sh'ma; a Journal of Jewish responsibility
1/17, October 8, 1971

SHI'UR FIVE: CHOSHEN MISPHAT

Sim shalom tova u-vracha chayyim chen va-chesed v-rachamim aleinu v-al kol yisra'el amecha. Barchenu avinu / Barcheinu imenu kulanu k-echad b-or panecha / panayich. Ki v-or panecha / panayich natata / natat lanu YAH eloheinu torat chayyim v-ahavat chesed u-tz'dakah u-vracha v-rachamim, v-chayim, v-shalom.

Grant peace, well-being and blessing, life, grace, love, and mercy for us and for all your people Israel.
Bless us, our father/mother, all of us as one, with your light.
For by that light of your presence, you gave us, YAH our God, the Torah of life, a love of giving love, righteousness, blessing, mercy, life, and peace.[1]

A starting place for a discussion of *Choshen Mishpat* is that *tz'dakah* / justice is God's gift to us, as the prayer above says. Its guiding principle is, *"Tzedek, tzedek tirdof /* **Righteousness, justice shall you pursue."**[2] Its desire is for *tzedek* for the *to'ein* / plaintiff and *tzedek* for the *nit'an* / defendant. Much of the subject matter of *Choshen Mishpat* is *hilchot to'ein v-nit'an*, people arguing with one another, complaining about each other. How do we decide who is the plaintiff and who is the one being charged? These are words and concepts with which we are familiar from secular law and they are the same terms and concepts here in Jewish law as well. *Choshen Mishpat* talks about damages and torts; who owes what to whom? Under what circumstances? What are the rules of evidence? What is the role of witnesses and what of documents? Where do you trust documents and where do you trust witnesses? How do you

---

[1] These are the words of the concluding blessing of the morning and, in mystical circles, the afternoon *amidah* as well.

[2] Deuteronomy 16:20.

constitute a *beit din* / court? All of this is the content of C*hoshen Mishpat*.

I have only a few things to say about *Choshen Mishpat*. My reason for having little to add in this area is that I came to the conclusion that the development of business law is much more advanced in the secular legal system than it is in *Choshen Mishpat*. To answer the questions of what constitutes a valid contract, what is a *sh'tar* / legal document, and what kind of *t'na'im* / conditions people place on their agreements, requires a level of sophistication that *Choshen Mishpat* does not meet. At this point at least, I don't know how to reconcile what we have in *Choshen Misphat* with the current state of business transactions and law in the secular world. To make Jewish law work again in a secular context, we need to do a lot of catching up. At this point, the best I can do is try and seed this process.

Recently there was a conflict between *Agudat Chabad* / the Chabad organization and the late rebbe's grandson. It concerned *sfarim* / holy books that belonged to the *Chabad* library and it became a court case. It wasn't handled by a *beit din*, by the arbitration method which is at the heart of the Jewish legal approach. Instead, both sides felt that they would be better served by the adversarial, but more sophisticated, approach of American secular law.

I'm not totally sure why this is so. I don't know why we can't do things, at least among ourselves as Jews, using the secular canons of evidence and combining them with a sense of *yosher* / what's right, which is the way our Jewish legal system goes about resolving conflict. We recognize that, while the letter of the law may favor one side over the other, sometimes that doesn't mean that there is equity and fairness. In our system, there is enough flexibility and trust given the arbiters so that they can make sure that law serves equity.

However, there are a few things I do want to say, at least for the purpose of beginning the process of revitalizing this area of *halachah*. For instance, one *s'michah* / rabbinic ordination I gave did empower the person with the traditional expression, *"Yoreh, yoreh* / Let him/her teach (or show the way)." In a traditional ordination, these words are usually followed by the areas in which the person is so empowered such as *"b-dinei issur v-hetter /* in the laws of what is forbidden and permitted." Then I continued with the traditional words, *"Yadin, yadin* / Let him/her adjudicate," to which I added, *"bi-p'sharot /* in compromises." In other words, when people go to court, then the rules are not those of *Choshen Mishpat.* Those rules work better when a rabbi says, "I will work with you, not as a regular *din torah* / bringer of a lawsuit to be adjudicated according to the laws of Torah, but I will work with you on a *p'sharah.*" A *p'sharah* means arriving at a conclusion that both sides can own either through mediation or arbitration. When a rabbi works from that point of view and is not restricted only to the *din* itself, then s/he is freer. The rabbi can then find out what the common practice in business is and help the parties arrive at a conclusion that is in keeping both with the fundamental principle of fairness which underlies Jewish law as well as being in harmony with current practice.[3]

This is one way to allow the subject areas of *Choshen Mishpat* to begin their adaptation to current realities. However, I still think that there may be too many obstacles preventing a process based on *Choshen Mishpat* from really taking hold. One reason is that the State of Israel has a legal system based on a hodgepodge of Turkish, British mandate, and Jewish law, along with the growing number of the legal decisions of Israeli courts, with one sitting on top of the other. In addition, Israel has to be part of the international community when it comes to commerce and it hasn't yet fully arrived at a way of dealing with law which is both its own and Jewish as well as in harmony

---

[3] See Talmud *Bavli Sanhedrin* 5b and *Rashi.*

with international practices. This is true not only for Israel, but all over the Middle East. For the most part, I think this has to do with using English common law as the language of legal conversation, which it seems to be in many parts of our world.

Another reason why it may be impossible for us to fully bring the legal areas of *Choshen Mishpat* up to date is the movement toward international courts where both individuals and governments are held accountable. I want Israel to be part of such an international system, which fulfills one of the seven Noachide commandments in a global way.[4] So my take is that in matters that have to do with business, we are better off accepting that *dina d-malchuta dina* / the law of the land is the law and to submit to the laws of the country and jurisdiction where we live.[5]

Having said that, I want to amplify what I said above and urge people involved in Jewish renewal to create alternatives to an adversarial court system where possible. I would call these *batei chesed u-p'sharah* / places of love and compromise, where agreements can be reached through mediation and arbitration. I have found that some issues are best resolved not through a court, where the focus is on assigning responsibility, nor in therapy. Because they have to do with what is *yosher* / equitable in a relationship, one should not have to work through layers of personality issues prior to reaching agreement. It's simpler and more productive for a couple to re-negotiate the ways in which they want to co-parent or even the way in which they want to be spouses by identifying and agreeing on what is equitable and

---

[4] According to Jewish tradition, the fulfillment of these seven commandments is required for gentiles to be considered righteous and worthy of a share in the world to come. One of them is to settle conflict through a system of courts.

[5] For example, the Jewish system of having three judges in a civil case and the secular one of having a jury of one's peers are different, but not in ethical conflict with one another. (ds)

fair. It's also the case that, should a *beit chesed* fail to be an effective mechanism for reaching this kind of agreement, it still leaves either therapy or the courts as a next resort.

I do believe that *batei chesed* should continue with the traditional practice of having a panel of three people who facilitate the process. From the point of view of *Kabbalah,* one represents *chesed,* the second represents *g'vurah,* and the third represents *tif'eret.*[6] Another way of looking at this is to invite the energies of the three patriarchs, *Avraham, Yitzchak, v-Ya'akov,* to be present. One says, "Hey, be kind." The second one says, "Hey, be strict." The third one says, "Do it with compassion." This is the deeper meaning of each disputant choosing one advocate and the two choosing the third, who then serves as a *machri'a* / the one who decides between them. Because of the odd number and the neutrality of the third person, there can't be a tie and the tie breaker is trusted by both sides.[7]

Years ago, when I was hoping to make *aliyah,* there were a number of projects I wanted to get involved with. One of these was what I would call a civilian *mikveh.* In Israel, most people have to spend some time in *milu'im* / the army reserves. Each time they go back into the army and then return to civilian life, there is a transition that would benefit from a ritual of initiation. Each reality requires different standards of behavior, yet when people are discharged from the army they go directly into the civilian population without having time to wash the army's rules from their systems and prepare to return to civilian life. One of the effects of these abrupt transitions is that the tone of voice in Israel has become more and more peremptory, more and more like a sergeant. People talk in an angry tone of voice which works in the military, but not in civilian life. That

---

[6] *Tif'eret* / compassion would be the mediator between the outpouring of love which is *chesed* and the rigor of *g'vurah.*

[7] The expression is, זה בורר לו אחד, וזה בורר לו אחד, ושניהן בוררין להן עוד אחד (Talmud *Bavli Sanhedrin* 23a).

was why I wanted to create a *mikveh* experience for people prior to their return to civilian society.

Closer to the subject matter of *Choshen Mishpat*, another thing I wanted to do was to create an inter-ethnic *beit din*. If an Arab Muslim had a dispute with a Christian, then the court would include a Muslim *kadi*, a Christian cleric, and a Jew who would then be the third. If the disputants were a Jew and a Christian, then the *kadi* would be the third on that *beit din*. In this way, the traditions would share their approaches to equity.

In that vein, I want to encourage us to have a number of people in each community who are willing to serve as *dayanim* / arbiters. When the dispute is between a man and a woman, at least one of the first two *dayanim* appointed would be a woman. These two *dayanim* would then agree on a third person whom they can feel they can trust for objectivity, for guidance, or for expertise in the particular field in which the conflict is taking place.

There is one other thing, on a deeper level, that I want to mention while we are thinking about *Choshen Mishpat*.

A young man once came to me and said, "Reb Zalman, would you guide me through something? Whatever path I follow here is going to create bitterness. Would you help me to make my way through this thicket with a minimum of karmic pollution?" I was deeply touched by the concept of working with a difficult choice in a way which produced a "minimum of karmic pollution."

If we want to heal this planet, then we have to learn to minimize karmic pollution. Some of it has to do with issues of forgiveness; some with issues of letting go of vindictiveness; and more has to do with not holding on to the need to win at any cost, to having "my way." If we keep the cycle of winning and losing, and each person wants to be vindicated in the end, then losing now only makes one want to win the next time. That means each side's karma continues to collide with the karma of others. One of the wonderful things about Yom Kippur and *t'shuvah* / **repentance** (or return) is that they are karma-stoppers. They allow us to let go and therefore stop our karma from bumping up against the karma of others. It's something like playing with the metal balls hanging by strings that hit one another. Because they are hard and directly in each other's path, once you start one or more balls swinging and hitting others, they can keep on going for quite a long time. If, instead of metal balls they were cotton tufts, they would continue to hit one another for a very short time and then stop. What we need to do is to remove the crazy energy that makes winning so important and replace it with something much softer and ultimately more satisfying.

This applies to the way in which we Jews relate to other religions. Deep inside I know that many of us still think, "Ah. Wait. *Mashi'ach* / **Messiah** will come and he will tell the Christians, 'It wasn't me that you thought you saw back then in Jerusalem. I haven't been here before.' It turns out that you have been lying all these centuries and we, the Jews, were right all along." What I now understand is we don't need *mashi'ach* if all s/he is going to say is that we were right all along. The purpose of *mashi'ach* coming, in whatever form that may take, is not for the final, triumphal vindication of any one faith tradition over others. Rather, *mashi'ach* comes for us all; because the truth is that none of us really has it all together. *Mashi'ach* will come because we all need redeeming, because we don't have it fully together and because we open to receiving Divine help. We will allow *mashi'ach* to come and be successful only when we all can let go of the need for vindication and, in so doing, reduce karmic pollution.

Finally, I want to say that we have to start looking at the issue of covenant again. I would like to invite people who are involved in law to help us learn to draw up contracts in such a way that they become a real *kritat brit*, a covenanting. Over the centuries, covenanting has become nearly lost and limited to the one ritual around circumcision. It needs *tikkun* / fixing, so that it can be expanded in the way it was during the biblical period. If we can renew what it means to enter into a covenant with another, I believe it will positively inform the recurring discussion we have about the need to continue circumcision, as well as how we celebrate the birth of daughters with true covenanting. Renewing covenant will have the overall effect of deepening the nature of our agreements and relationships.

Choshen Mishpat
Appendix: Sacred Controversy

[In the preceding chapter, Reb Zalman discussed the way in which a *beit din*, applying the primary value of *yosher*, could still be useful today in helping people reach resolution of disagreements and conflicts through mediated agreements. Here, we offer four texts which focus on *yosher* and its application in places where a single, exclusive conclusion is not possible. Ownership of the resolution by the involved parties and the sense that differences of opinion are seen as parts one related whole, are the common threads linking these texts.]

Talmud Bavli Sanhedrin 5b

רבן שמעון בן גמליאל אומר:

הדין - בשלשה, ופשרה - בשנים.

ויפה כח פשרה מכח הדין. ששנים שדנו - בעלי דינין יכולין לחזור בהן, ושנים שעשו פשרה - אין בעלי דינין יכולין לחזור בהן.

רש"י: שהרי נתרצו, ועל פיהם עשו

Rabban *Shim'on ben Gamli'el* says:

Judgement – [requires] three, compromise [between the litigants] – [requires only] two. Compromise is to be preferred over judgement. If a judgement is rendered by only two judges, the litigants can renege on the decision [and request a new trial in front of a "full" court], but if two arrive at a negotiated settlement – then the litigants have no further recourse Rashi: Because they themselves arrived at the agreement and it wasn't imposed on them.

Talmud Bavli
(Soncino Translation;

Chullin 116a
Interpretation by Daniel Siegel)

רבי יוסי הגלילי אומר: נאמר
לא תאכלו.

R. JOSE THE GALILEAN
SAYS, IT IS WRITTEN, YE
SHALL NOT EAT OF
ANYTHING etc.

מאי איכא בין רבי יוסי
הגלילי לרבי עקיבא?...
איבעית אימא: עוף איכא
ביניהו,

What is the difference
between the views of R. Jose
the Galilean and R. Akiba?...
You may say, the difference
between them is as regards
fowls: R. Akiba maintains
that wild animals and fowls
are not included in the
prohibition of the Torah but
are prohibited rabbinically,
whereas R. Jose the Galilean
maintains that fowls are not
even prohibited by the rabbis.
There is also [a Baraitha]
taught to the same effect: ...
In the place of R. Jose the
Galilean they used to eat
fowl's flesh cooked in milk.

ר' עקיבא סבר: חיה ועוף אינן
מן התורה - הא מדרבנן
אסירי,

ור' יוסי הגלילי סבר: עוף
אפילו מדרבנן נמי לא אסיר...

תניא נמי הכי:...

במקומו של רבי יוסי הגלילי
היו אוכלין בשר עוף בחלב.

This text illustrates how much is really at stake in Talmudic disputes and how controversy is treated by the rabbis. We have here not just two disputants, Rabbis Akiba and Jose, but also "the Talmud." It is "the Talmud" which reports that the difference of opinion is in fact about something of substance and not just apparent. "It" then goes on to demonstrate anecdotally that what it believes is the true nature of the dispute in fact manifested in real life; Rabbi Jose's followers actually ate fowl with dairy. Thus, before any effort is made to decide which of the two rabbis is correct, a third party to the conversation, "the Talmud," plays its own role by "helping" the disputants clarify their disagreement and better understand each other. As a person trained in the skills of conflict resolution, I recognize this as very similar to the role I play when I mediate. The purpose of this activity is to help the parties arrive at a mutually agreeable resolution of their problem by helping them to understand each other, appreciate the consequences of not finding a solution, and by emphasizing the valuable relationship they share.

Looking at a passage in *Pirkei Avot* /Ethics of the Fathers can help to make this more clear. "Every controversy that is for the sake of heaven will have lasting value. Controversy which is not for the sake of heaven will not endure" (5:20). At first glance this might seem strange, for why would one want any controversy to endure? Yet, in mediation, that is exactly what happens. If the parties focus on what will happen "from now on," appreciate and understand each other's positions, and acknowledge the importance of their relationship, then they can agree to disagree over the facts of what happened while still coming to an agreement over what the *halachah* needs to be for them from now on. My own experience demonstrates that such outcomes are possible even when the stakes are very high.

Rabbi Menachem Mendel of Vitebsk was one of the early Chassidic *olim* / emigrants to Palestine in the years immediately following the death of Rabbi Dov Ber, the *Maggid* of Mezeritch. His teachings are collected in a book called *Pri ha-Aretz* / Fruit of the Land. From his discussion of this same passage in *Pirkei Avot*, I extract the following lesson: Each of us, as Judaism often teaches, is a world in miniature. Thus, we are the site of the interplay of the six spheres representing the major forces whose dynamic interrelationship and balance is this universe. These include expansive love / *chesed*, power and focus / *g'vurah*, mercy and grace / *tif'eret*, perseverance / *netzach*, beauty / *hod*, and physical/sexual energy / *y'sod*. All these interact with each other in the field of this world, called the kingdom / *malchut* which is *Sh'chinah*, the divine indwelling, and which, according to Mendel Vitebsker, is also the human being. Thus, each of us is a part of the divine it/herself. The way in which we make our behavioral decisions depends on which of the spheres we believe best channels the transcendent divine energy needing to manifest in the world at a particular moment. That decision-making process, the weighing of whether to be inclusive or exclusive, lenient or strict, is a dispute for the sake of heaven. The meetings between us become the meetings of one divine energy with another, and the awareness of the divine transcendence is the unifying force. On the other hand, when we externalize this process and see the other, not as a part of the divine and thus of ourselves, but rather as the embodiment of falsehood as we become the embodiment of truth, then this is a dispute which is not for the sake of heaven and it should be discontinued immediately. In the language of conflict resolution, it needs to be reframed into one which is for the sake of heaven.

The experiences we have shared over the past decades, not only the holocaust but the powerful effects of modernity itself, the changes in social and economic structure, the failure of material plenty to result in true happiness, and the end of the fixed and solid universe in the relativism of Einstein, have been profoundly unsettling. And if Job could question the justice of God based on his personal experience, why not any and all of us? If Rabbi Levi Yitzchak of Berditchev could "sue" God over the treatment the Jews were receiving in his day, is it not obvious that any survivor of the camps could also do so? Our certainties over the correctness of our positions, be they on the traditional or the liberal side, only mask the deep insecurity and confusion we are really feeling within. A dispute for the sake of heaven is not defined by the subject matter of the dispute. Rather, and this is what makes controversy sacred, it is defined by the way in which we conduct that dispute. What endures is this process of determining the correct balances of divine energy appropriate to each moment within the context of the covenantal relationship with God which we all share. My prayer is that we can learn to approach each other again acknowledging how much we need each other, how troubled we all feel, and how much we would gain from engaging in disputes for the sake of Heaven.

מגיד דבריו ליעקב נ"ח
Maggid D'varav L-Ya'akov 58
(Dov Ber, The Maggid of Mezeritch)

אלו ואלו דברי אלהים חיים בין האוסרים ובין המתירין.

These and these are the words of the living God, both for those who forbid and those who permit.

דבדעת חדרים ימלאון, כל המדות הם באים מכח הדעת.

"By knowledge are its rooms filled (Pr. 24:4)" - all the attributes derive from the power of *da'at*, knowledge.

רצה לומר מחמת שאני יודע שהוא אוהבי אני אוהב אותו, ומחמת שאני יודע שיש גדול ממני אני בוש ונכנע ממנו ומכבדו, וכן כיוצא בזה.

What this says is that because I **know** that the other loves me, so I love him/her; and because I **know** that there is someone greater than I, I submit before that person and his/her honor, and so with other similar examples.

וכל אחד המשיך ממדת הדעת שיהיו הצירופים של הדיבורים כך וזה כך,

שזה המשיך ממדת הדעת מדת אהבה שיהא הביצה מותרת, וזה המשיך מהדעת מידת יראה והביצה אסורה.

וכשאחר רצה לשנות את ההלכה כמו רבי יהושע דאמר אין משגיחין בבת קול, החזיר את הדין הזה למדת דעת. ומשם המשיך את הדין למדה אחרת והמשכיל יבין.

And each one is drawn from the quality of *da'at*, such that the combinations of speech turn out this way and that.

This one draws through *da'at* a loving quality which allows the egg (laid on a holiday) to be permitted, and this one draws from *da'at* through caution and forbids the egg.

And, when one needs to change the law, as Rabbi Joshua did when he said that we don't pay attention (even) to a divine voice, one is returning the discussion to *da'at*, and from there it can be drawn again through a different quality, as the intelligent will understand (by themselves).

EPILOGUE

I want to return to some words written by Rupert Sheldrake because they provide a framework for understanding how *halachah* evolves, and then I want to conclude with some words of caution.

When Sheldrake was asked what his theoretic foundation is, he said,

> The theory of formative causation is concerned with how things take up their forms, or patterns, or organization. So it covers the formations of galaxies, atoms, crystals, molecules, plants, animals, cells, societies.

> What we call life, a living being, is a self-organizing system.

> An atom doesn't have to be put together by some external agency. It organizes itself. A molecule and a crystal are not assembled by human beings bit by bit, they spontaneously crystallize. Animals spontaneously grow. All these things are different from machines which are artificially put together by human beings.

I see the *taryag mitzvot* / 613 commandments as also being an organic system, something which grows itself in a complex relationship with its inner programming and ever-changing and evolving environment rather than being something which is put together like an erector set. Sheldrake continues,

> So, what my theory is concerned with, is with self-organizing natural systems, and it deals with the cause of form. And the cause of all these forms I take to be organizing fields, form-shaping fields, which I call morphic fields, from the Greek word for form...The original feature of what I'm saying

is that the forms of societies, ideas, crystals and molecules depend on the way previous ones of that kind have been organized. There's a kind of built-in memory in the morphic fields of each kind of thing. So the regularities of nature I think of as more like habits, than as things governed by external mathematical laws that somehow exist outside of nature....

[T]he idea is that each species, each member of a species draws on the collective memory of the species, and tunes into past members of the species, and in turn contributes to the further development of the species...

That is what I've been saying about *halachah. Halachah* is the field in which we live with one another. Another form of the same word as *halachah* is *ta'halich* / process, which becomes the name of the way, the field in which we are with each other.

Then if you say, "Well, what is it that all fields are made of?" the only answer that can be given is space-time, or space and time.[1]

In other words, field is the name for the space-time location within which the "thing" or the subject happens. Field is the way in which they relate to each other. Gravity, for example, can be thought of as a field. As I wrote earlier, "In the world of *p'shat*, in the world of *domem*, of physical things, what does it mean to say that God loves or that God is love? Two bodies in space attract one another. Thus, in *olam ha'asiyah* / the world of action, gravity is love." The field about which we are talking in the world of halachic discourse compares with the way gravity is a field in the physical world. And a field is nurtured by the way in which things happened before.

---

[1] http://www.levity.com/mavericks/rupert.htm

Sheldrake also compared the regularities of nature to habits rather than to obedience to laws arriving from the outside. Things happen now in a certain way because this is how they happened in the past. Thus, there is a way in which the template of the next stage of becoming is shaped by the habits of the past.

A little later, he says that DNA does not mandate the shape of the next phase. DNA determines what ingredients will be used to construct this form, but how they shape it depends more on what this organism has learned in its evolution. Applying this to *halachah*, my take is that we have to remember and remain able to keep our field together.

Let me share another quote:

> So in the case of a potato, you'd have a whole background resonance from past species of potatoes, most of which grow wild in the Andes. And then in that particular case, because it's a cultivated plant, there's been a development of a whole lot of varieties of potatoes, which are cultivated, and as it so happens potatoes are propagated vegetatively, so they're clones.

> So each clone of potatoes, each variety, each member of the clone will resonate with all previous members of the clone, and that resonance is against a background of resonance with other members of the potato species, and then that's related to related potato species, wild ones that still grow in the Andes. So, there's a whole kind of background resonance, but what's most important is the resonance from the most similar ones, which is the past members of that variety. And this is what makes the potatoes of

that variety develop the way they do, following the habits of their kind.

Usually these things are ascribed to genes. Most people assume that inheritance depends on chemical genes and DNA, and say there's no problem, it's all just programmed in the DNA. What I'm saying is that that view of biological development is inadequate. The DNA is the same in all the cells of the potato, in the shoots, in the roots, in the leaves, and the flowers. The DNA is exactly the same, yet these organs develop differently. So something more than DNA must be giving rise to the form of the potato, and that is what I call the morphic field, the organizing field.[2]

Based on this, our question becomes, "If *halachah* has a morphic field, then what can anybody do consciously and deliberately to design it?" Doesn't *halachah* have to develop like potatoes, like the rabbinic saying, *"puk chazi mai ama d'var* / go and see what the people do;"[3] let's see how it's going to develop. These forms develop spontaneously and you can't interfere with them. You can't design myths. You can't design this kind of progress; it unfolds or it doesn't. If you try to work with it consciously it becomes artificial.

I bear witness against that point of view. I say that the way in which we use our minds to restructure things is also part of the unfolding of the morphic field. Once we are human, once we accept the idea that we have or at least share responsibility, once we talk about *kabbalat ha-torah* / receiving and accepting Torah,[4] once we invoke the principle, *"ki lo ba-shamayim hi* / it is

---

[2] http://homepages.ihug.co.nz/~sai/shel-int2.htm

[3] Talmud *Bavli B'rachot* 45a.

[4] See Talmud *Bavli Shabbat* 88a for the idea that the Jews completed the process of accepting Torah only in the days of Mordechai and Esther.

not in heaven,[5] once we say that the *da'at ha-kahal* / **agreement of the community** is very important here,[6] we shape the field and the field shapes us. Together, we and the halachic process constitute the field.

Another way of looking at this new developmental stage of Judaism in general and *halachah* in particular is to think about it in the stages represented in the words of the *Shabbat* morning service and which I discussed elsewhere in more detail.[7] The new paradigm into which we are entering can be called *efes bilt'cha* / **there is nothing but You.**

The first major stage in our development could be called "*ein aroch l'cha YAH eloheinu ba-olam ha-zeh* / **there is no comparing You, YAH our God, to anything else in this world.**" This was in the age of Aries where God and human beings are seen as so different from one another. Then we entered the consciousness of "*ein zulat'cha malkeinu l-chayei ha-olam ha-ba* / **there is no one but You, our Sovereign, for life in the world to come.**" This was when we were saying there is a *n'shama* / **soul** and there is a *guf* / **body** and, while there is a parallelism they share, they are two different beings. Now we are entering the place where we are saying, "*efes bilt'cha go'aleinu li-mot ha-mashi'ach* / **there is nothing but You, our redeemer, in the days of** *mashi'ach*; everything is God. It's all God, godding endlessly.

Therefore, I say that our minds' God-ing is also at the service of the planet. It is not just an invention. Our being together, our thinking together, form the process of the field itself. In fact, that's what the field of studying *Torah* has been through all these generations. People have put their heads together to work things through. And we trust that somehow the *Sh'chinah* will find a way of influencing the totality.

[5] See Deuteronomy 30:12 and Talmud *Bavli Bava M'tzi'a* 59b.

[6] See Talmud *Bavli M'gillah* 7a and the formula preceding *Kol Nidre*.

[7] *The Kabbalah of Tikkun Olam*, pp. 42-43.

I want to give you a *b'rachah* for this process in which we are involved together: Be blessed to be open on the inside to hear the *ru'ach ha-kodesh* / holy spirit that operates in you, so that what you create is truly what is needed. This is how it was for the *anshei k'nesset ha-g'dolah* / men of the great assembly, who had to say that the time of the *n'vi'im* / prophets who received their messages directly through inspired visions is over. They understood that *ru'ach ha-kodesh* now would be accessed through our caring, our minds, our tradition, and our transmission. It says, "*Heim amru sh'loshah d'varim* / They said [only] three things."[8] But what they said became *Torah*. So, I pray that what you say will also become *Torah*. Trust that process and then say what you are called to say, not from the place of your "ouches," from the place of your knee-jerk reactions, from the place of the angers and the hot-spots that you have inside of you, but from the place where you can be in touch with that field and with the *ru'ach ha-kodesh*.

This means that it's really important for this generation to wash out as many of the "hot potatoes" as possible from our way of thinking. I know in our family there were these hot potatoes that my grandmother passed on to my mother and that my mother passed on to me. When I was sixty, I did the Fischer-Hoffman Process, the Quadrinity Process, in order to learn to wash out some of these things so that I didn't hand them on to my children. I also made an arrangement so that any of my children or grandchildren who want to do a process like that will get help so that what we do can be *l-dorotam* / for generations to come.

In this generation, we all are in some way *t'mei'ei meitim* / ritually affected by contact with death. We have been touched by holocaust and we are still polluted and impure because of it. We need to do extra work to remove this impurity from our

---

[8] Mishnah *Avot* 1:1.

systems so that we become better instruments for *ru'ach ha-kodesh* doing its work with us. So, please, continue this conversation with each other, deeply and honestly, over the course of the next many years, so that what we are doing now will indeed be *l-dorotam.*

Remember, while on the one hand it is said, "*Lo alecha ha-m'lachah li-g'mor* / It is not for you to complete the work," and that applies to me and to you, it also says, "*V-lo atah ben chorin l-batel mi-mena* / Neither are you free to absolve yourself from this work."[9] We can't finish it, absolutely not. But I do hope that in this book I was able to put some "software" at your disposal by sharing how I think about these things, so that you might find your own ways to enter into this field so that it works for you. Then you, too, will become part of this amazing process which began so long ago and will continue for a long time to come.

---

[9] Mishnah *Avot* 2:16.

Printed in the United States
by Baker & Taylor Publisher Services

Printed in the United States
by Baker & Taylor Publisher Services